Personnel Management for the Smaller Company

Personnel Management for the Smaller Company

A HANDS-ON MANUAL

Linda A. Roxe

A Division of American Management Associations

Library of Congress Cataloging in Publication Data

Roxe, Linda A
    Personnel management for the smaller company.

    Includes bibliographical references and index.
    1. Small business--Personnel management. I. Title.
HF5549.R67   658.3'03   79-10867
ISBN 0-8144-5509-3

© 1979 AMACOM
A division of American Management Associations, New York.
All rights reserved.
Printed in the United States of America.

First Printing

To the bottom line

PREFACE

Most smaller businesses do not need a personnel director. Every business does need a personnel function—a systematized approach to hiring, paying wages, developing benefit programs, training and developing personnel, establishing guidelines for employee behavior and discipline, record keeping, and timekeeping. Before hiring one person, an employer should know how to recruit and select that employee, the job requirements, vacation and other time-off benefits, working hours, and how to enforce guidelines for employee behavior.

This book is intended as a "hands-on" guide to establishing sound personnel practices. It is meant to raise questions, present alternatives, and offer help in solving personnel management problems. There are few footnotes or references and no graphs. I have tried to reduce theory, technical material, and background information to a pragmatic and digestible form that can be used by any manager charged with the personnel function of an organization.

It has been my experience, both as a consultant and as a personnel executive, that prospective planning is just as important in dealing with human relations situations as it is in any phase of the production process or financial management. In fact, personnel have a considerable impact, both as assets and liabilities, on the bottom line. This book is intended to help you increase personnel assets and decrease personnel liabilities. It is written from my own experiences and designed to help every employer who wants to avoid penalty charges for improper timekeeping records, excessive overtime expenditures, back pay judgments, and discrimination suits. It is meant to help you utilize your human resources effectively while maintaining a good employer-employee relationship.

LINDA A. ROXE

CONTENTS

1 THE BUSINESS OF PEOPLE

People cost money. Recruiting, training, and compensating workers can be the largest single item in an employer's budget. People also *make* money by producing the goods or services that yield income or fail to make money by failing to produce. Given the sizable financial investment required to employ people and considering worker impact on production, it is clear that people affect the bottom line of every enterprise. Thus it seems reasonable and necessary, from an internal perspective, to place a priority on the efficient management of human resources. External circumstances reinforce that view. Legislative, technological, economic, and social developments during the past two decades have revolutionized the employer-employee relationship as well as the attitudes with which people approach work.

The Civil Rights Act of 1964 has significance beyond its provisions, which in themselves have sweeping import. The law, with its accompanying publicity, triggered a concern for individual rights that has permeated a broad spectrum of activities. In the employment milieu an aggressive federal enforcement agency, the Equal Employment Opportunity Commission (EEOC), state and local organizations, and private-interest groups have provided enthusiastic and accessible resources to grievants. The resulting legal activity has created a block of decisional law that requires a continuous updating of information and has made the personnel function quasi-legal in nature. Subsequent laws like the Equal Pay Act have had similar effects on personnel management.

Technological advances have increased the amount and accessibility of data used to plan and conduct business activities and,

1

in many industries, the complexity of the production process. As a result, the structure and content of many jobs have been changed, and training or adjustment has been required on all levels of employment. Problems have arisen when mechanization has eliminated jobs or changed them so radically that workers have been displaced and skills made obsolete. Technological advances also have increased the speed, impact, and circulation of communications and thereby broadened the experiences and exposure of individuals. Hence, the world is smaller, competition is fiercer, and people are better and more immediately informed as well as geographically and socially more mobile.

Economically, there has been an inflationary spiral that has pinched employer and employee alike, often causing confrontation and hostility rather than empathy. On the one hand, workers face about a 6 percent increase in prices each year; on the other hand, employers face the same decline in purchasing power plus the problem of meeting employee wage needs. Economic growth has slowed; the balance of payments has been unfavorable; government spending is increasing; the stock market has seesawed; there have been surges of high unemployment. Even very large corporations have had cash flow problems and have faced financial crises, and some have failed. All those developments have created insecurities and pressures and have changed the attitudes and needs of both employee and employer.

However, it is perhaps social changes, some of them resulting from economic, technological, and legislative developments, that have had the largest impact on the employer-employee relationship. Increasing geographic mobility, developments in communications media and transportation, the increased employment of women, and similar influences have changed the structure and nature of family relationships. There is a tendency for individual family members to participate in discussions and decisions, and there is a greater sense of independence among family members. The adoption of less structured teaching techniques and student participation in the selection of courses and study material, as well as in classroom discussion, have reinforced the democratic trend. Hence, persons entering the labor market have an innate sense of independence and have come to expect similar opportunities to participate.

Then too, people have developed new values—ecological concerns, energy conservation, consumerism, political and social reform, and activism. Thus the college students of the fifties, chided for being apathetic, were followed by a group in the sixties who took to the streets to demonstrate and demand. Although somewhat more subdued and conventional in their techniques, the seventies group nonetheless have developed strong values and a spirit of activism that extends into the employment milieu.

Perhaps the most traumatic of the social developments of the past two decades are the widespread increases in alcoholism and the use of drugs. Although alcohol abuse has been a long-standing problem, its increase has magnified production losses because of increases in absenteeism, higher accident rates, and related employee relations problems, as well as declines in health, stamina, and work quality. The problem has become so extensive that employers have been forced to recognize and deal with the problem openly.

A newer source of concern stems from the use of drugs, which not only presents the work-related problems associated with alcoholism but also involves serious legal penalties. Although marijuana, amphetamines, "uppers," "downers," tranquillizers, "speed," heroin, and other addictive substances have a deleterious effect on judgment and skills and build up user dependency, narcotics abuse is more difficult to detect than alcoholism and is very difficult to prove.

Those factors have made the business of employing people more complex than hiring and firing and expecting employees to follow directions in return for a pay check. Applicants for jobs demand information about company antipollution plans; political radicals attempt to infiltrate and disrupt production in target companies; union members reject negotiated settlements; minority groups demand better opportunities; workers clamor for more meaningful and demanding work; employees publicly criticize company policies and managers to clients and potential clients; reverse discrimination suits are filed; managers question traditional methods of conducting business.

Those trends require management first to recognize their existence and understand their causes and then to work constructively within the framework of existing conditions. Both within the traditional personnel functions and in the development of a structured plan for the management of work and worker, there is a need for balance and rational creativity in personnel management.

PERSONNEL FUNCTIONS

The personnel management function can be divided, for convenience of discussion, into four subfunctions—employment, compensation, employee relations, and training—all of which contribute in a very real way to the management of people at work. Each function is discussed from an operational standpoint throughout the ensuing chapters. They are capsulated in this chapter to describe their value as management tools from the perspective of internal operational needs and in light of external demands.

Employment

The employment function is concerned with staffing from two perspectives: the acquisition of competent personnel and the control of staffing expenditures. People must be recruited, screened, and placed according to the needs of the organization. The implications and demands of that deceptively simple job are numerous, as can be seen from a simple listing of the requirements:

1. Knowledge and development of recruiting sources for a wide range of personnel from file clerk to manager and the ability to attract qualified applicants from those sources.
2. Timely filling of vacancies to maintain staffing at levels needed for production.
3. Knowledge of jobs, job specifications, job requirements, and job-related problems within the organization.
4. Interviewing prospective employees and verifying credentials.
5. Placement of qualified candidates by matching credentials with job specifications and personalities with personalities.
6. General information about the overall functioning of department and organization, including goals, philosophies

of management, positions on controversial issues, benefit and salary structures, sales or production figures, and any other question an applicant is likely to ask.

7. Enthusiasm for the company, one's own job, and applicant prospects.
8. Interpersonal skills to establish quick rapport and elicit information from applicants and deal with line managers.
9. Budget control to maintain staffing at appropriate levels of numbers, expertise, and salaries as defined by management.
10. Public relations skills to foster employer image among the various publics, including the community and potential clients.
11. Legal knowledge to avoid discriminatory practices and the appearance of discrimination within the function, among sources, and by line supervisors.
12. The development and implementation of affirmative-action plans, including outreach recruiting and staff education.
13. The creation of internal employment opportunities and appropriate disposition of transfer requests, promotional systems, and the like.
14. Turnover analysis and prevention.

In the light of economic and legal demands, the personnel function, even in the small organization, must be approached with precision, organization, planning, and expertise.

Compensation

There is no question that the compensation function is concerned with spending money rather than making it. However, the expenditure of money to pay wages and purchase employee benefits is necessary to attract and retain the employees whose production will yield income. Within that frame of reference, the focus of the compensation function is to spend monies wisely, that is, to control expenditures and secure the best value for them.

Value, or investment return, from a wage-and-salary program stems from the ability of the program to attract qualified personnel within the marketplace, meet the reasonable expectations of the employees, and reinforce production activities. People often view their earnings worth in terms of the amount of money they might reasonably expect to make by performing a similar job for another employer and in terms of co-workers' salaries. Therefore, it is necessary to establish a wage structure that pays occupations at rates comparable with those paid by other employers in the community and that reflects the comparative worth of jobs within the organization. In addition, raises should be correlated with employee production and performance.

Benefits, including vacations, sick leave, holidays, and insurance programs, should be planned to reflect community standards, meet the needs of the workforce, reinforce the employer-employee relationship, and provide the best coverage and service for the lowest price. Service, particularly as related to claim processing of insured benefits, is a key to obtaining the maximum employee relations value in the benefits area.

The compensation function should control expenditures in three ways: policy enforcement, cost containment, and adequate budget planning. Since wage-and-salary administration involves not only the design of pay structures but also the implementation of related policies, the enforcement of those policies also falls within this functional jurisdiction. Thus any related transaction, including timing and amounts of raises and correlation between increments and performance, should be monitored.

Similarly, cost containment with respect to benefit expenditures and claims experience generally is a responsibility of the compensation function. In that respect the timely processing of new enrollment and benefit changes, as well as payroll deduction forms, is key. Analysis of health insurance, workmen's compensation, and unemployment compensation claims, vacation utilization, and control of sick leave abuse fall into this category. Development of remedial programs or incentive plans also can be assigned to this function.

Within its parameters as a staff function, the compensation area is charged with developing statistics to be used in budget preparation and analysis. That includes information on cost-of-living projections, anticipated merit increases, premium expenditures, and the like. The point is to anticipate increases in compensation-related expenditures so financial planning can be accurate.

Training

Training programs should be developed to increase production by increasing worker skills, efficiency, and stability. In addition to general orientation of new employees and initial job training by supervisors or training specialists, the training function can fill employee and organization needs in many areas: advanced or additional skill training, supervisory and motivation techniques, management development, and general-education or other special programs. Such needs can be met by in-house training, tuition assistance, scholarships, or just referral service for outside training or education, professional seminars, and the like.

The charge is to teach and update skills to improve production techniques and provide job satisfaction as well as to develop personnel to meet future organizational needs. Again the key is to insure value for the investment of dollars and training time.

Employee Relations

The maintenance of a positive relationship between management and labor is essential to optimal production, staff stability, and the prevention of work disruption. Although the ongoing employee relations process is both a staff and a line obligation, the responsibility of the personnel management function is first to create the framework by developing rules, policies, and procedures regulating employee behavior and discipline and then to monitor their implementation by line supervisors. In addition, the function is a vital link in management-labor communications and bears responsibility for the formation and maintenance of record-keeping systems.

Essentially, people on all levels of the employment scene need to be treated reasonably and equitably. Hence, the prospective establishment and enforcement of rules and procedures is an essential part of employee relations. The thrust is to provide objective standards for employee behavior on the one hand and appropriate means of dealing with deviations from those standards on the other. As far as possible within the frame of human response, discipline should be uniform throughout the entire organization.

The establishment of structural lines of communication available to employees as well as management is key. Systems for handling employee grievances and questions, obtaining employee feedback and involvement, and providing counseling are vital. The personnel function often acts as a resource to both line supervisors and employees in meeting such needs.

The record-keeping responsibilities involved in the employment of people are numerous. Internally, in addition to personal data, records are required to document credentials, employment and salary history, time off, discipline, performance, and insurance enrollment. There are also legal requirements for records associated with employment and personnel, timekeeping, agency reports, tax and immigration purposes, and pay periods. The design and maintenance of record-keeping systems fall to the employee relations function.

In summary, the thrust of the personnel management function is to promote the goals of the organization by quality staffing, by the control of wage, benefit, and staffing expenditures, by effective training, and by the establishment of a well-ordered and motivational work environment and staff stability.

Organizational Structure

Organizational structure is concerned with the functional division of work within the organization as a whole and within each department. As a work-planning tool it is valuable because it allocates work and inhibits duplication of effort. In the area of personnel management it is valuable because it creates parameters of responsibility and authority in terms of assignments and levels, delineates reporting mechanisms, and establishes the basis for interfunctional relations.

The first step in creating a structure for the organization as a whole is the analysis of the functions that must be performed to achieve the goals of the organization. That is accomplished by listing the functions, grouping them into logical order, and assigning them to specific operations and individuals.

The example shown in Figure 1 represents the functional organization of a small consulting firm which is staffed by two partners, a full-time secretary, and a part-time researcher-

Figure I. Functional organization of a small company.

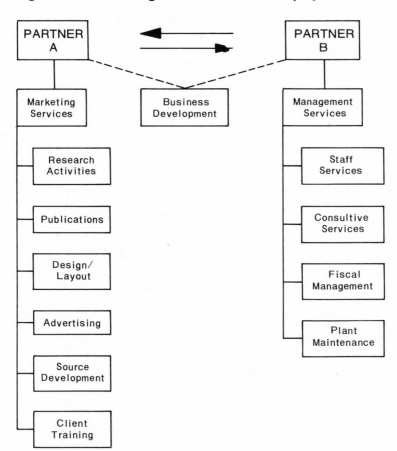

writer. The firm also subcontracts some assignments or parts of assignments to other consultants with whom it maintains close relations. It acts as management agent, general management consultant, and/or marketing consultant for its clients. Since one partner is a marketing expert and the other has a background in general and financial management, the two have divided their functional areas of concentration accordingly. Both share responsibility for developing the business and obtaining new clients, and the partners have a close planning and working relationship.

Figure 2. Functional organization of a manufacturing plant.

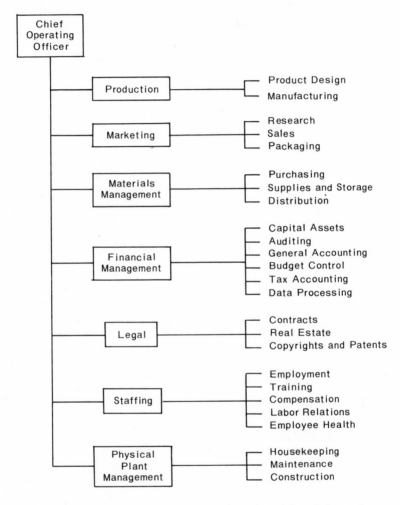

Figure 2 shows the same kind of functional breakdown for a manufacturing plant in which the size and nature of the enterprise make the functional organization complex. It is important to note that the function delineations shown are part of the initial step; although they will influence the development of the structure, there is much room for manipulation. It may be desir-

Figure 3. Reporting organization of a small company.

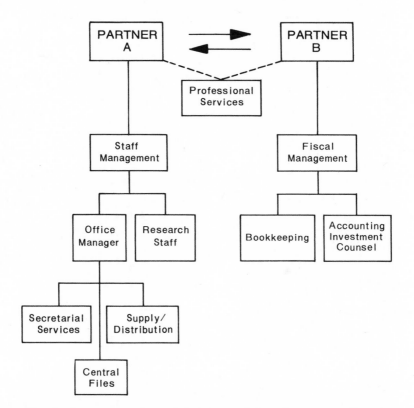

able, for instance, to have the personnel function report directly to the corporation president in one organization, but in another, to have an administrative vice president to whom personnel, materials management, and legal service report. (Compare the arrangements shown in Figures 3 and 4.)

Such decisions are made by assessing the complexity of the functions and the expertise of key personnel. It is necessary to achieve an equitable and reasonable distribution of work and to utilize effectively the expertise and energy of key executives, including the chief executive. For instance, to have too many functions reporting directly to the president of an organization erodes much of that executive's time by involvement in too many

Figure 4. Reporting organization of a corporate office.

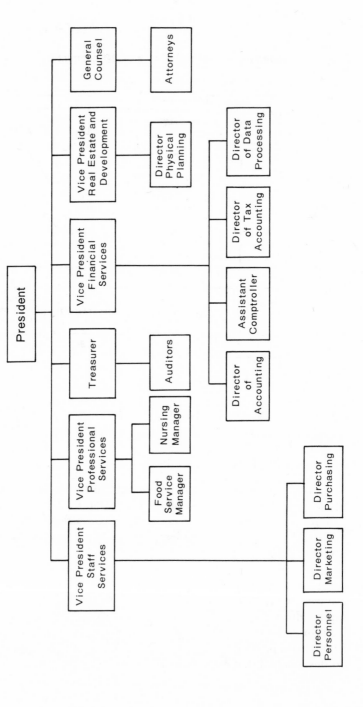

of the day-to-day activities of individual departments. The president should be able to concentrate on long-rane planning, results, and problems that require personal attention.

Departmental organization is developed in much the same way. First, the functions of the department are analyzed, and then a structure is developed. The process begins with a listing of tasks that must be performed and a grouping of the tasks into a logical order to delineate jobs. In some instances there should be an overlapping of duties to provide adequate coverage and "relief staffing" for breaks, absences, vacations, and temporary work peaks.

Staffing should be a measure of the nature of the work to be performed, the numbers of work units involved in the work, the complexity of work units, and the schedules to be met. The nature of the work obviously will determine the expertise needed to accomplish the job—typing, accounting, law, engineering, or whatever. The workload plus the complexity of the work will determine how many people are required.

The schedule of demands will determine staff schedules. It is one thing, for instance, to note that insurance premiums must be calculated; how many such calculations must be performed and the complexity of the calculations, straight or split rates, will determine actual needs. In some instances staffing also must reflect demand for services. More X-rays, for instance, are taken in a hospital during the morning shift when routine and special procedures are scheduled than at night when only emergencies are handled. Similarly, banks will have more customers transacting business on paydays, Fridays, days before holidays, and lunchtime.

From these data reflecting function, numbers of employees, and scheduling requirements, the departmental organization is developed. As with the structure of the overall organization, attention must be given to efficient manpower utilization, sound reporting systems, and cost. Figure 5 shows the departmental organization of the data processing function for a corporate organization. The separation of individual functions is necessitated by a heavy and diverse workload, particularly in clerical areas. The seemingly top-heavy structure is required because the department is in the formative stages and an unusual

Figure 5. Departmental structure of a data processing function.

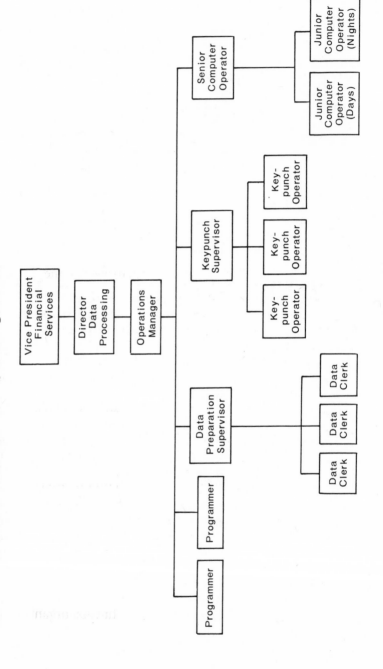

amount of professional expertise and monitoring is needed to meet production goals.

One point should be stressed. Organizational structure should be dynamic. That is, it should be modified to reflect the changing needs of the organization that result from technical or personnel changes. However, frequent and large-scale reorganizations will have a negative effect on personnel morale and production. Any changes in reporting relations or organization should be explained to workers. Care should be taken to review the substance of the modifications, the reason for the change, and the expected advantage.

SUMMARY

The management of people at work has been growing more complicated owing to increasingly complex production processes, economic conditions, legal restraints, and especially changes in social values, standards, and behavior. As a result, there is a need for a new focus on personnel management techniques. Efficient employment procedures must be developed with an emphasis on compliance with civil rights legislation and cost control. Compensation functions must focus on effective spending.

Training must equip workers to meet management production goals and derive satisfaction from employment. Employee relations techniques must be utilized to create a motivational work environment and maintain a positive management-labor relationship. In addition, work functions should be structured to promote efficiency and establish appropriate reporting relationships.

2 THE EMPLOYMENT PROCESS

The best-known and most visible personnel function is that of interviewing and hiring. The employment process starts when the need to hire is established and continues as applicants are attracted, screened, interviewed, and selected or rejected. However, a systemized approach to staffing requires more than the surface activities. It involves a method for monitoring the size and occupational level of staff, budget control, forms, procedures, selection criteria, and standards. Even in the small office, where the approach is likely to be less formalized, attention ought to be focused on such details.

POSITION CONTROL

Position control is a system for assuring that staffing does not exceed budget limitations. The best way to control such personnel expenditures is to keep a running record of current staffing compared with authorized or budgeted levels. Although the need for a mechanism of this type increases with the size of the organization, position control can be effective for monitoring personnel activity, recording a history of employment growth, and managing department growth even in the smaller business.

The System

The format of the position control system can vary from a simple listing of budgeted positions versus staff on hand to a computerized report. The important point is to establish a graphic form and to keep it current. One simple format is shown in Figure 6; it includes, on a department basis, each authorized

Figure 6. Position control chart.

DEPARTMENT: Accounting — Payroll

POSITION: Supervisor	BUDGETED HOURS: 40			CUMULATIVE HOURS: 40	
NAME	START DATE	HOURS	CURRENT WAGE	PROJECTED WAGE	REVIEW DATE
Smith, Carol	4/1/70	40	5.20	5.45	4/1/77

POSITION: Payroll Clerk	BUDGETED HOURS: 120			CUMULATIVE HOURS: 120	
NAME	START DATE	HOURS	CURRENT WAGE	PROJECTED WAGE	REVIEW DATE
Green, John	5/3/71	40	3.51	3.69	5/3/77
Brown, Jill	7/14/72	20	3.37	3.57	7/14/77
White, William	8/18/72	20	3.25	3.42	8/18/77
Black, Winifred	3/29/76	40	2.90	3.05	3/29/77

POSITION: Typist	BUDGETED HOURS: 20			CUMULATIVE HOURS: 18	
NAME	START DATE	HOURS	CURRENT WAGE	PROJECTED WAGE	REVIEW DATE
Jones, Jon	10/16/75	18	3.00	3.15	10/16/76

position and the number of hours per week budgeted for that position (excluding overtime). All current employees in those positions are listed along with the number of hours they have been hired to work. Much additional information can be included: start dates, performance review dates (most recent and next scheduled), current salary, projected raises, data for reports to the Equal Employment Opportunity Commission. The chart is updated every time a transaction occurs—hiring, termination, raise, leave without pay, and so on.

A Kardex file system can be used to provide a fingertip staffing history for each department along with a history of each position and employee in the department. It can be as simple or as complex as needs dictate. The simplest approach would be to list on a large index card the authorized complement of each department starting with the department head or supervisor and ending with the lowest-ranked position:

MAIL ROOM

POSITION	BUDGETED HOURS
Supervisor	40
Assistant Supervisor	40
General Office Worker	40
Mail Distributors	140
Microfilm Clerk	20

That card would be followed in the file by an individual card for each employee showing position, name, start date, salary and position history, and any other convenient information:

4/15/74	Start—Microfilm Clerk	2.15
7/15/74	Performance Review	2.26
4/15/75	Performance Review— Promotion: Mail Distributor	2.46
6/30/75	Leave Without Pay	—
8/30/75	Return from Leave	2.46
6/15/76	Performance Review	2.58

MAIL DISTRIBUTOR   SMITH, HARRY   20 HRS.

Cards can be designed to contain social security number, address, insurance information, performance review rating information, termination information, and other pertinent information. Some organizations find that a convenient way to keep reference files on former employees so the entire file can be stored without using the limited space needed for active records.

Although their availability often depends on programming limitations and the accessibility of computer time, computer-generated reports can provide much position control data. Minimally, reports should include a list of authorized positions, in-

Figure 7. New-position authorization.

Job Title _____ Department _____
Salary Grade _____ Salary Range _____
Start Date _____ Hours _____
Previously Budgeted Position?   New Job Description Required?
   Yes ☐   No ☐   Yes ☐   No ☐

Status: Full Time ☐   Part Time ☐   Permanent ☐   Temporary ☐   Until ☐

Job Specifications _____
_____
_____
_____

Justification for Addition _____
_____
_____

_____   _____
Department Head   Date

_____   _____
Authorizing Signature   Date

_____   _____
Authorizing Signature   Date

cumbents, and each employee's current salary information. When need dictates and resources allow, much additional information can be included—salary ranges, projected increase dates and amounts, past increases with dates, position authorization dates, a breakdown of authorized hours, overtime data, year-to-date budget, and expense figures.

Position Authorization

In any organization, financial authority and responsibility are well defined and often quite limited. Since personnel costs are a major expenditure, it is usually practical to have a policy that defines the authority to approve new positions or substantive changes in function. If so, a system should be devised to obtain and document necessary authorizations before any recruiting is begun. A sample form for the purpose is shown in Figure 7.

FORMS

Well-designed forms are important not only to establish records pertinent to employment activities but also to foster the communications necessary for efficiency and coordination throughout the process.

APPLICATIONS. Obviously, applications are an important part of the interview process, since they provide the framework which will shape the interview. Whether purchased or specially designed, the employment application form (Figures 8 and 9) should conform to certain criteria:

1. Format. The form should be arranged logically, and sufficient space should be available for an applicant with normal-sized handwriting to fill in all the information requested.

2. Content. The form should request enough information to provide a capsule of the applicant's work history, educational background, and skills. Spaces for names, addresses, and telephone numbers of previous employers and supervisors, as well as appropriate dates and titles, should be included.

3. Reference authorization. Each applicant should sign a statement authorizing verification of his credentials. If consumer reports are used, appropriate releases should be incorporated (see Chapter 9).

4. Legislatively required information. The application form is a logical means of obtaining information required by federal and state governments such as the social security number, which often is needed to check references. In addition, employers are required to insure that noncitizen employees hold visas which permit them to work. Other individuals may be subject to licensing requirements. In rare instances the law may prohibit the hiring of individuals who have been convicted of certain types of crime; for example, banks are restricted from hiring people convicted of felonies.

5. Legislatively prohibited information. The application should require no information that can be construed as contributing to discriminatory hiring practices. Each state has specific legislation prohibiting inclusion of certain questions, and, of course, federal civil rights legislation forbids asking questions regarding sex, age, religion, race, or national origin. (For discussion of the subject, see Chapter 9.) It is a good idea to

Figure 8. Employment application form (front).

Name_____ Phone_____ Date_____

Address_____
　　　　　　(STREET)　　　　　　(CITY)　　(STATE)　　(ZIP)

Date of Birth_____ Social Security No. _____

If not a U.S. citizen, type of visa_____ Visa No. _____

Emergency or Alternate Contact_____
　　　　　　　　　　　　　　　(NAME)　　(ADDRESS)　(PHONE)

Education/Training: Please list all relevant information, including military training, special courses, seminars, etc.

	Name and Location	Dates From	To	Major Subjects	Degree Diploma
High School					
College					
Other					

Describe licenses or certificates held _____

Typing speed_____ Shorthand_____ Dictaphone_____

Other Skills (specify) _____

_____

Name of relatives in Company employ: _____

Have you ever worked for Company before?_____ Dates_____

Job Title_____ Reason for leaving _____

Who referred you to Company?_____

Do you have any physical disabilities that would affect employment?

Describe_____

"An Equal Employment Opportunity Employer"

Federal law prohibits discrimination on the basis of race, creed, color, national origin, sex, or age. The information requested on this application is necessary for conformance with federal record-keeping requirements and is intended for no other purposes.

Figure 9. Employment application form (reverse).

Work History: Include U.S. Military as employer					
Name of **Present** or **Last** Employer				Phone Number	Address
Starting Date Month Year	Leaving Date Month Year	Starting Pay	Final Pay		Reason for Leaving
		Supervisor		Title	May we contact
Job Title and Description:					

Name of **Next Previous** Employer				Phone Number	Address
Starting Date Month Year	Leaving Date Month Year	Starting Pay	Final Pay		Reason for Leaving
		Supervisor		Title	May we contact
Job Title and Description:					

Name of **Next Previous** Employer				Phone Number	Address
Starting Date Month Year	Leaving Date Month Year	Starting Pay	Final Pay		Reason for Leaving
		Supervisor		Title	May we contact?
Job Title and Description:					

I authorize this company to conduct an investigation of my application. I understand that any false or misleading information furnished by me on this application form or in connection with my application for employment may result in rejection of the application or termination of employment. I also understand that any employment given me will be on a 90-day probationary basis.
Signature_____ Date____

(Personnel Use Only)
Interviewer comments (Personnel) _____

Interviewer comments (Department)

Start Date	Job Title	Grade	Salary	Authorization	
				Signature	Date

include on the application form a statement of open-hiring practices.

6. Interviewer's comments. Documented records of interviews are important. There should be space on the application blank to provide a permanent and convenient record of what transpired during the interview and why the applicant was or was not considered for a position.

INTERVIEW RECORDS. It may be advantageous, especially in the larger organization with several interviewers, to keep a flow sheet listing the applicants interviewed, jobs applied for, source, disposition, sex, and origin (Caucasian, black, American Indian, Spanish-surnamed American). Such a system, which is recommended by the Equal Employment Opportunity Commission, may be helpful in several ways. Discriminatory referral patterns can be documented and corrected before a problem develops. For instance, if interviewers tend not to refer or department heads tend to reject minority applicants, there will be graphic evidence of discriminatory attitudes. The failure of certain recruiting sources to produce an appropriate mix of applicants can be seen easily. On the other hand, the interview records will provide ongoing documentation of nondiscriminatory hiring policies and practices should an individual allege otherwise.

At the same time, a flow sheet will provide many data for in-house use. For example, the ratio of interviews to hires will help in analyzing the effectiveness of interviewers, identifying the employment agencies who screen well and those who do not, gauging the local labor market, and measuring the general effectiveness of such sources as advertising and employee referrals.

In the area of budget management, a flow sheet will provide data for an analysis of the effectiveness of recruiting dollars. For instance, if two employees are hired from a $150 newspaper ad and then two others are recruited through agencies at a cost of $1,000, the latter sum may be excessive. However, if fifty interviews were conducted before the two people were hired from the ad and only two interviews were conducted to employ the individuals referred by the agency, the time expended might be an equalizing factor.

REQUISITION FORMS. In a multidepartment organization, it is usually helpful to have a requisition system to initiate recruiting. The form should include title, reason for recruiting (new position, replacement, and so on), department interviewer, skills and personal requirements, hours, and desired start date. In most cases it is best to require an authorizing signature as in the sample shown in Figure 10.

RECRUITMENT

Successful recruiting—that is, the attraction of qualified applicants—is essential to staffing any operation. Far from being an easy task, recruiting can be difficult and in some cases is a very competitive endeavor. There are three particular facets that should be discussed: timing, sources, and advertising.

Timing

When to start recruiting is a question with many implications. The decision should reflect the individual situation with respect to a number of considerations.

ACTIVITY. If for some reason business is slow or staffing needs are temporarily lower, it may be advisable to defer recruiting so long as other employees can handle the workload without disruption of service or severe loss of morale. On the other hand, a peak in activity demands accelerated recruiting efforts.

LABOR MARKET CONDITIONS. In a community with a limited labor market, recruiting should be initiated as soon as a vacancy is anticipated.

CYCLICAL VACANCIES. If there is a history of turnover at certain times of the year, staffing needs should be anticipated and recruiting started ahead of time. Often when a community includes a college or university, resignations can be expected at the end of the school year; in an area near a military base, resignations can be anticipated when the annual transfers are announced.

TRAINING PROBLEMS. Predictably high turnover occupations that require training before the employees can function may necessitate recruiting early enough to train a "class" before a staffing crisis occurs.

EXPANSION. When expansion is planned, recruiting should be scheduled to allow staff increases timed to meet work demands without incurring unnecessary expenditures before the additional income can support the salary expense.

Figure 10. Job requisition form.

Job Title _____ Department _____ Interviewer_____

Start Date_____ Grade_____ Salary Range _____ Hours _____

Reason for Recruiting: New Job_____ Authorization Date _____

Replacement for _____, Who Is: Terminating ☐ On Leave ☐

Promoted to _____ Effective Date _____

Status Papers Have ☐ Have Not ☐ Been Processed

Status: Full Time ☐ Part Time ☐ Permanent ☐

Temporary ☐ Until _____

Position Specifications: _____

_____

_____

_____

_____   _____
Authorizing Signature   Date

(reverse)

Recruiting Authorization
(Personnel)
Date Received_____   _____   _____
                                Initial   Date

REFERRALS

Date	Applicant	Interviewer	Disposition	Rejection Reason

THE NATURE OF THE JOB. When a key employee is to be replaced, recruiting should begin as soon as possible. It may be desirable to have some overlap of employment to provide a smooth transition.

Source Development

The most effective recruiting source will depend on location, size, budget, turnover, and the nature of the organization. It is important to be aware of alternatives.

EMPLOYEE REFERRALS. In many cases employees will be the best advertising. Employee referrals can be encouraged by posting a list of openings in active employee areas such as sign-in sites, bulletin boards, and lounges. Some companies pay a bonus when a new employee is hired through an employee referral; partial payment to the referring employee can be made when the applicant is hired and the balance at the end of the probationary period. However, discretion should be used in *relying* on employee referrals. First, referrals should not result in unintentional discrimination against minority groups. Second, hiring relatives can result in personnel problems, particularly in a smaller organization or when two or more family members report to the same supervisor.

PUBLIC AGENCIES. Potentially, public agencies are excellent sources of applicants. However, they must be evaluated on an individual basis. In larger communities and urban areas public agencies sometimes are staffed by people who have an overabundance of clients and little training in interviewing, skill evaluation, and placement; the staff may have no experience in business and no solid understanding of the listed jobs. Often applicants are unskilled individuals whose unemployment benefits are conditional on registering with the agency. Some agencies are better staffed and more oriented to training and counseling. In addition, some public employment offices that specialize in placing particular groups such as veterans, the handicapped, or those with special training provide excellent service.

In any case, job orders should include explicit information about the job specifications and requirements. It is appropriate to insist that referrals be made only by prearranged appointments and to question the interviewer about the applicant's work history and experience before accepting a referral. There is no reason to deviate from valid job selection standards or to waste interviewing time.

PRIVATE EMPLOYMENT AGENCIES. Private employment agencies can be an excellent source of referrals, particularly to the small organization with limited interviewing time. Moreover, they have a financial interest in providing good service, particularly if repeat business is likely. However, it is important to have a good understanding of how the private agencies work.

Generally, private agencies attract applicants through newspaper advertising designed to bring into their offices the largest possible number of placeable persons. Therefore, they tend to advertise the kinds of jobs that will appeal to the group they are trying to reach. Although many people will find such jobs appealing, few individuals are the right match for the jobs. Some of the people who are not qualified for the advertised job will be told about another great job and that employer will be told about fantastic applicants who are interested in his job. In other words, the goal of the employment agency is to sell the job to the applicant and the applicant to the employer.

If a referral results in a placement, there is a fee, usually a percent of the annual salary. Depending on the area, labor market, state of the economy, and unemployment, the employer may be expected to pay the fee. In areas where employer payment is customary or usual, the number of referrals will be lower and the quality of applicants will be less than first rate if the employer does *not* pay the fee. That is simply a supply-and-demand situation.

It is advisable to be selective when using private agencies. The classified advertising section of the newspaper will reveal which agencies advertise jobs most realistically. Other employers or employees can relate their experiences with agencies. It is best to limit the number of agencies used and to develop workable relationships with them.

Complete and realistic descriptions of the job and the kind of person required to fill the job are essential. Again, it is best, before accepting referrals, to prescreen applicants by getting a detailed history of each applicant's experience and skills. It is helpful to know the fee schedule and the guarantees an agency offers before hiring through it. A copy of the agency contract will provide important insight into its operations.

Another point to be aware of is that the applicant has signed a legally binding contract before being referred. If an applicant responsible for his own fee defaults on payment, he will be called on the job; the employer will be advised by the agency of delinquent payments and possible garnishment of wages, and the employer's aid will be solicited. A terminated employee may still be responsible for the fee.

SPECIAL-INTEREST GROUPS. Groups such as the National Alliance of Businessmen, NAACP, Urban League, professional associations, and various rehabilitative and vocational agencies often have excellent placement services that should be explored.

SCHOOLS. Schools are excellent recruiting sources and are always glad to be able to help place their graduates. The guidance offices of high schools and the placement offices of colleges, junior colleges, and commercial schools often are the typical contacts. Some institutions offer specialized curricula such as a two-year business administration course in which accounting is emphasized and health-care training. Basic carpentry and mechanical skills are taught in trade schools.

REHIRES. Rehiring former employees who were good is recommended. When such an employee leaves, the door to reemployment should be left open.

PREVIOUS APPLICANTS. A cross-file of previous applicants is a helpful device. There are many times when potentially good applicants are not hired because there were no appropriate vacancies or there was a surplus of good applicants at the time they completed applications. A simple index card file can be kept for each position, and in it potential applicants can be listed for easy location of their application forms in the alphabetical file when an appropriate position becomes vacant.

Effective Advertising

Advertising can be an extremely effective way to attract applicants, and is often economical in the long run. Like any other tool, however, it must be used effectively.

TIMING. It is essential to time advertising to reach the greatest number of likely candidates. The pattern of other advertisers can be seen in the classified section of the local newspapers. If the classified section is consistently larger on a certain day, for instance Sunday, that is usually the best day to advertise. In certain areas it may pay to advertise several days a week—Sunday and Tuesday or Sunday, Tuesday and Wednesday; in others the extra expense is wasted. It is fine to experiment on a small scale, but it is not always wise to be swayed by a package deal or cheaper weekday rates.

WHERE TO ADVERTISE. For the most part local newspapers are the best bet. It is helpful to ascertain the newspaper with the largest circulation or the largest classified advertising section. Newspapers in certain communities may reach a specific labor market such as blue or white collar workers or professionals. There might be a large nearby city that is a good market for potential employees. Professionals or management employees might be apt to consult the business sections of the newspapers in key cities. Special-interest newspapers, professional journals, association magazines, and newsletters also are good sources.

DESIGNING AND WRITING ADVERTISING. Ads should be compatible with the general style of the publication, but they should stand out. Economy is important; to sacrifice results for a slight saving is false economy. Effective advertising includes both words and eye-appeal—copy and layout.

1. Copy. *Brevity* is key. Both job and organization should be sold. Position requirements should be specific. Image is important. No one looking for a job wants to wade through deathless prose. People want to know that the pay is good and benefits are super, or free parking is available, or the office is over a train station or is modern, or that there are 55 holidays a year, career advancement opportunities, and 25 free coffee breaks a day.

Employers want applicants with particular skills who are available for the midnight shift, have 25 years of experience, and have degrees in alphabetical science engineering. It never hurts to use advertising to create the image desired in the community or among potential customers, clients, or future applicants. If management philosophy stresses professionalism, community service, personnel development, progressiveness, national scope, research orientation, environmental safety, or whatever, that philosophy should be included in ads for some levels of employees.

Practicality is essential. Certain jobs at certain times in certain areas will attract more applicants than can be handled. If this response is anticipated, the ad should include restrictions: limited interview hours, résumés only, or interview by appointment only. Neither the applicant nor the staff will be helped by a mob scene or unreasonable telephone response.

2. Layout. The classified advertising section of a local newspaper is a good guide to layout. Some ads stand out and others get lost in a blur of monotony. The difference lies in the use of space and type size.

Space is important to size and design. Obviously, a large ad stands out either because it is long or because it occupies a double column. But space can be handled very effectively merely by judicious use of white space, such as by inserting an extra line of white after a job title or company name, or by arranging copy with margins and/or indentations like a business letter or formal invitation.

In most cases type size is used to good effect in headings, job titles, catch phrases preceding the ad, or the company name and address. Organizations that are large or prominent in the community might find it beneficial to emphasize name. In other cases the job or catch phrase should be set in large type. The body of ads usually is set in agate or one-line type size. Two-line type can be used to make an ad longer and lighter to the eye or to set it off from most of the ads on the page.

LEGAL IMPLICATIONS. To comply with Equal Employment Opportunity guidelines it is important to observe the following.

1. There should be no reference to age or sex. It is unlawful to use "young," "boy," "girl," "man," "second man in department," "a right-hand man," and so on. It is better to use such words as "individual" and "person" or a specific job title such as maintenance mechanic (not maintenance man) or office assistant (not Girl Friday).
2. Help Wanted—Female or Help Wanted—Male classifications should not be used.
3. Each advertisement should include the phrase An Equal Employment Opportunity Employer M/F.

ADVERTISING AGENCIES. Depending on the organization's size, inclination, frequency of advertising, and location, an agency that specializes in classified advertising can write and place ads. Such an agency can offer advice on trends, circulation, artwork, timing, and, occasionally, later deadlines. It can be particularly helpful for advertising in out-of-town or professional publications or for display advertising.

Advertising agencies can help save money if they are used correctly. A frank discussion of advertising budgets or limitations is always helpful, and inquiry about the price of each ad can be made before placement is authorized. Agency financial arrangements vary. Sometimes the advertiser pays only the normal advertising fee and the agency is given a rebate by the publication; in other cases the charge is a percent of the publication fee. Artwork is a separate cost item.

SCREENING AND INTERVIEWING

The importance of effective screening and interviewing in the hiring process is obvious, but it is equally important to maintain a good public relations image while achieving that goal. The public relations aspects of the process are far-reaching.

A person's initial impression of any organization often results from his contact with the person who greets him or interviews him in the employment office. The successful candidate's first impression—the efficiency and courtesy with which he was treated—will color his attitude toward his job. The applicant who is screened out also will remember how he was treated. If he was received with courtesy and dignity, he will walk away disappointed that there was no appropriate vacancy—but without a feeling of hostility and rejection. It is worth the effort to maintain a good community image and avoid charges of discrimination. "Being rude may get you sued."

Screening

The screening process is a positive function which involves screening in applicants who are qualified and not merely screening out those who clearly are not. Because the aim is to choose the best candidate from a group of qualified applicants, all those individuals must be sold on the organization so that they will begin the interviewing process with a positive attitude. At the same time, to interview every individual who inquires about job availability would waste the time, and often money, of applicants unqualified for current vacancies, short-change the qualified applicant who might become disenchanted, and harry the poor interviewer, who would have to rush interviews and gloss over other functions.

One of the most important assets in any screening program is the person who handles routine inquiries. Such an individual should like people and have a high tolerance for different kinds of personalities and lots of interruptions. The busier the employment function, the greater is the need for a good sense of humor.

The screener must be kept informed about what positions are available or expected to become available and the basic requirements for those positions. The screener and everyone connected with the employment process must be trained to know the requirements of civil rights legislation and company hiring policies, affirmative-action plans, and so on.

It is essential that all inquiries be handled with honesty. Available jobs must be acknowledged. Callers can be questioned about work experience, education skills, and the like. If qualifications are in line with job requirements, callers should be encouraged to present themselves for interviews. Definite appointments shoud be set up; the address should be confirmed; and, if necessary, directions or the location of the office should be given.

Callers or applicants whose qualifications do not match job requirements are more difficult to handle. They should be told specifically what qualifications are lacking. If qualifications are minimal, it may be helpful to state that other respondents have tended to have better credentials. The key is to treat people with honesty, dignity, and tact—in short, to disqualify them on object-ive grounds without rejecting them as personalities.

Although it is possible to discourage them from applying for a job, applicants cannot be prevented from completing applications. If no position is available, no interview is required. People can be told that applications will be kept on file, and they should be advised whether it is customary to review such applications when vacancies occur. If vacancies are infrequent, it is helpful to tell applicants so. When a position is available, any individual who wishes to apply for it should be interviewed unless it is clear that the applicant does not meet objective criteria—lacks eligibil-ity for licensure, does not have secretarial skills, mechanical training, or whatever.

Employers have a right to interview by appointment only; it is not necessary to be on call to interview anyone who walks in. Interview appointments can be set up, or individuals can be requested to call later or schedule appointments. Employers are not obliged to review any previously completed applications whenever vacancies occur. Neither are they obliged to mail applications, provide baby-sitting services, or extend interviewing hours to accommodate people.

Interviewing

An interview is an opportunity for the interviewer and applicant to exchange information so that each can make a judgment concerning the desirability of making or accepting an offer of employment. On the one hand, the interviewer must secure information concerning the applicant's qualifications, preferences, and aspirations and then try to match that information with the conditions existing in the organization; on the other hand, the interviewer must provide the applicant with information concerning the job, working atmosphere, salary, benefits, and potential so that the job seeker can measure his needs against the potential employment situation. Thus the interviewing process is most important to both parties and should be pursued with care.

PREPARING FOR THE INTERVIEW. Prior to any interview there should be a thoughtful analysis of the vacancy and a careful study of the applicant's application or résumé. The job should be reviewed with respect to not only the job description and specifications but also the problems of the department. If there has been high turnover, job specifications may need revision. There may be a need to match an applicant with a supervisor with a difficult personality. Or there may be a requirement for a person who can keep up a certain pace, handle pressure, or whatever. The interview should then be geared to match the applicant with the job situation as well as the job specifications.

A close perusal of the application may point to areas that should be emphasized during the interview—a job that is particularly related to the vacant position, a work pattern, an educational experience. The application is not unlike a road map: even though all the intersections are marked, it is helpful to establish a route before starting to drive.

WHERE TO INTERVIEW. All interviews should be conducted in

an office or private area where the applicant will feel free to speak candidly. During the interview there should be no interruptions or disruptions such as telephone calls or personal visits.

WHO SHOULD INTERVIEW. It is imperative that anyone involved in the interviewing process be specifically trained in interviewing techniques, be familiar with hiring policies and affirmative-action programs, and know the legal implications of civil rights legislation, EEOC guidelines, and court decisions. Although it is usual and practical to have a department or individual responsible for screening and initial interviews, the department head or immediate supervisor also should interview any serious candidates.

CREATING RAPPORT. Since the purpose of interviewing is to get to know the applicant, it is most important to make the applicant feel at ease so that he will be himself. The interviewer should make him feel welcome and comfortable by offering him a chair, asking how he is, adding a *brief* amount of small talk—the weather, traffic, or whatever.

Interview Techniques

The point of conducting an interview is to get information about the applicant; therefore, the most important technique is listening. The interviewer must concentrate on the applicant and hear what he's saying—and not saying. The following is a list of interview do's and don'ts.

1. Do use plain language—easily understood words, not polysyllabic words or technical jargon. It is best to choose words that will have the same meaning to both the interviewer and the applicant.
2. Do avoid fine distinctions. Don't split hairs or get hung up on insignificant details.
3. Do be brief. Don't use long or multiple-part questions. Several short questions will be more effective.
4. Do place the stress in the proper place. Emphasis on one part of a question or phrasing questions in a way that leads the applicant will color the response.
5. Don't make assumptions. Don't assume that an applicant is well versed on a subject. The emphasis should be on finding out what he knows.

6. Don't use a pencil too often. An applicant will not be comfortable if he thinks every word is being recorded. Notes should be few and brief; it is better to make notes immediately after the interview.
7. Don't show approval or disapproval. The applicant will stop talking or try to please the interviewer who reacts visibly.
8. Do be objective. Personal likes or dislikes should not influence judgment.
9. Don't be impatient or give an applicant the impression that he is being rushed or not being given a fair chance.
10. Don't prolong an interview. If it is clear early in the interview that the applicant does not meet the requirements of the job, don't go into unnecessary detail; instead, hit the highlights. Keep the pace unhurried and steady, but don't waste time.
11. Do concentrate on the applicant's experience and knowledge. Ask about his likes and dislikes with respect to his previous job.
12. Do ask open-ended questions that will encourage the applicant to talk instead of giving one-word answers.
13. Do ask specific questions—why he chose a certain field of endeavor, why he left his last job, how he reacted to certain situations or would approach a problem, what he thought of his co-workers or boss on his last job.
14. Don't pry into an applicant's personal affairs, but don't hesitate to ask personal questions if necessary. For example, if an applicant states he left a previous job because of marital difficulties, ask whether those problems have been solved but *not* the nature of the problem.
15. Don't ask questions that can be construed as discriminatory. Avoid questions that relate to race, religion, age, color, sex, or national origin. That includes asking about previous garnishments, arrest records, military discharges, child-rearing problems, marital status, and the like.

EXPLAINING THE JOB. This is a key part of the interview. It will allow the applicant to judge whether the job appeals to him and open up a new line of questioning for the interviewer—has he ever typed letters, had that kind of responsibility, used that kind of system? In addition, it will give the interviewer an opportunity to observe the applicant—whether he reacts positively and enthusiastically, whether he asks questions and seems to be genuinely interested or says he might as well give it a try for a few days. For certain jobs it may be helpful to have the applicant read a job description. It is a mistake to sell the job or insist that an applicant will like it. Such practices often result in short-term employment.

TOURS. If there is genuine interest in him, the candidate should be shown his potential work area. That will help him to identify with the organization and to get a good feel for the job. Certain candidates might be given a tour of the physical plant or parts of it so that they can have a comprehensive picture of the function of the organization as a whole as well as a clear picture of departmental interaction.

Testing

There are as many approaches to testing as there are tests and test developers. There are aptitude tests and personality tests, intelligence tests and achievement tests, psychological tests and skill tests; there are puzzles and inkblots and graphs and equations and pins and devices galore. Volumes have been written on the use of tests in employment screening, including some far-reaching court decisions. But the whole topic can be boiled down to two considerations: whether the test(s) will accomplish employment goals and whether the program meets court-established guidelines. The most any test can do is provide additional information to help in the selection process. Test results should be only one part of the picture and should not be given more importance than other selection criteria; they cannot replace the interview, reference checks, or educational or personal qualifications.

Test Selection

There are many "canned" tests that have been designed to measure general aptitude and intelligence. Most of them test verbal and mathematical skills as well as general knowledge and are designed to determine accuracy and speed. Such tests can be particularly helpful in filling jobs that require individuals with a great deal of mental ability. However, a less sophisticated approach to testing may suit the situation by providing specific data and job-related knowledge.

For instance, in hiring a secretary, typing speed should be tested, but accuracy and the ability to space correspondence properly also are important. A secretarial applicant who will have to use a dictaphone or shorthand or compose routine correspondence should be tested in those areas as well. A file clerk might be asked to arrange names or numbers in logical sequence. Someone who will be working with figures might be asked to perform basic calculations similar to those required by the job. In such tests the emphasis would be on accuracy instead of speed, although starting and finishing times of applicants should be noted and compared.

Test Validity

Although it is relatively simple to justify the use of job-related tests, especially if the tests come close to duplicating job situations, formal testing programs are the object of much scrutiny. Although the Tower amendment to the 1964 Civil Rights Act specifically approves the use of professionally developed tests that are not intended or used to discriminate, employers are obligated to guard against unintentional discrimination resulting from the use of employment tests. EEOC guidelines,* while no longer requiring universal test validation, state that tests must be validated if a selection rate for any minority is less than 80 percent of the group with the highest selection.

In some instances tests have been used with such consistency throughout a particular industry that their validity has already been established. Those tests may be available through trade associations or similar special-interest groups. Employers may validate testing programs themselves, but the procedure can be complex. Current employees can be tested, and then pertinent performance review factors, such as quantity and quality of work, accuracy, production, and judgment, can be correlated with the test scores. If that approach is not possible or desirable, the test can be administered to all new hires for a period of time and the test results can be compared with performance review

* "Uniform Guidelines on Employee Selection Procedures," *Federal Register,* Dec. 30, 1977.

data and length of service. All scores must be examined to ensure that there is no significant difference in test results for any minority group. If any group does score lower than the norm, the test is invalid.

It is important to administer all tests in a quiet area where there will be no distractions or interruptions. Applicants should be told that the test is only one factor in the employment decision, and employees should be reassured that no tests administered for validation purposes will have a bearing on their job statuses. Equal Employment Opportunity Commission offices will be glad to provide any available information.

SELECTION

The next step in the employment process is the selection of applicants. That is often difficult, particularly when there are a number of candidates from whom to selert or when demanding jobs are being filled. It is important to hire the person who most closely meets job requirements, but it is necessary to establish accurate and valid criteria for making employment decisions. Once the decision has been made, there is one other related issue: communicating the decision to both successful and unsuccessful candidates.

The Decision

In most cases the prospective supervisor or department head will make the final decision about who should be hired. The closer the work relationship, the more important it is to look for compatibility. Therefore, even if a higher authority actually makes the decision, it is important to involve the supervisor. When peers will be expected to work closely with the newcomer, it is a good idea to have them meet the candidates before an employment offer is made. But in addition to personal compatibility, there are a number of points that should be considered to focus on the whole rather than attach undue importance to any one factor.

JOB KNOWLEDGE AND EXPERIENCE. If an individual will be expected to function at a certain level, it is important that he have the specific knowledge and experience demanded by the job—technical expertise, command of office procedures or bookkeeping principles, typing skills, familiarity with a computer model, or supervisory experience. Someone without the appropriate background might be capable of doing the job but would require additional training and the time to learn.

LEVEL OF INTEREST. The candidate's expressed interests and expectations must match the opportunities available in the employment situation. If there will be little opportunity for advancement or intellectual growth and stimulation, it may be better to hire a less-bright person who has the ability to perform the function but does not have aspirations that cannot be realized in the organization. That is particularly true in dealing with overqualified candidates—college graduates who apply for clerical jobs or accountants who seek bookkeeping work—or in filling routine jobs, such as assembly line positions, or dead-end jobs from which there is no logical line of progression without substantial amounts of training—nurses' aides, orderlies, mail clerks. In addition to creating potential high-turnover situations, a practice of hiring overqualified applicants with the idea of advancing them may be discriminatory if there is a pattern of rejecting minority applicants who otherwise would be qualified. Bona fide job requirements would have to be established to justify such a practice.

PHYSICAL ABILITY. The point in establishing physical criteria is not to discriminate against the handicapped, but to match a candidate's physical ability to valid job requirements. The objectives are to protect the individual from dangerous situations, eliminate turnover, reduce workmen's compensation expenditures, and conform to Occupational Safety and Health Administration (OSHA) safety standards. Thus an individual with an active back problem should not be hired to do a job that requires constant lifting; people with leg or foot problems may not be able to stand constantly; and individuals with poor reflexes or manual dexterity will not be able to operate certain mechanical equipment safely. On the other hand, a blind person with good typing skills may make an excellent dictaphone typist or receptionist; an employee with a hearing impairment might be an asset in a job requiring intense concentration; mentally retarded individuals can be trained to perform many routine tasks.

WORK HISTORY. The candidate's employment record is an important index to be considered. If there has been a history of short-term employment, the reasons must be assessed—failure to perform satisfactorily, lack of training, boredom, dissatisfaction with working conditions, or inability to get along with co-workers or superiors. If there is an established pattern, it is wise to consider whether the applicant has been at fault and whether circumstances in the proposed job will alleviate or reinforce the problem. If an applicant is being considered for a key position, a history of progressive responsibility and salary is important.

PERSONAL CHARACTERISTICS. Every job situation includes special demands that must be met. In some instances employees will be required to work under pressure or at an accelerated pace. There may be an uneven workload with peak and slow periods. If public contact is involved in a job, individuals must be able to get along with people or, in some instances, a certain kind of people—the very young or very old, the handicapped, the rich or the poor, intellectuals, aggressive salesmen, or the temperamental.

One person might be expected to work under close supervision and another to function independently. If there is a difficult supervisor or a situation in which a person must report to more than one superior, there are special problems. There might be restrictions based on safety or security considerations that would rule out an applicant with a personal idiosyncrasy such as heavy smoking. These are valid working conditions against which applicants should be measured and about which they should be told so they can assess the situation and their own willingness to adapt to it.

REFERENCES. References are an important means of verifying information and gathering data about job candidates, but they are only one criterion. It is important to remember that the people giving references are only human. An otherwise satisfactory employee may have had a legitimate personality conflict with a supervisor; a supervisor may have considered a resignation to be a personal affront; there are legitimately poor employment situations; and there are former supervisors who are in the midst of bad days. On the other hand, many former employers are afraid or hesitate to give a truthful reference if the response is other than glowing.

At least two references should be checked, and, if possible, former supervisors should be consulted personally. Questions should be specific—how often was the employee absent or late, what were his duties, what were the dates of employment, what were his strong *and* weak points. The candidate's eligibility for rehire and the supervisor's enthusiasm or lack of enthusiasm for rehiring the person are important. If the applicant is not eligible for rehire, the reason should be determined.

It is usually better to make reference checks by telephone so that a real exchange can take place. However, some employers will not give information by phone. If that is the case, a letterhead form can be used to request information on employment dates, job responsibilities, quality of work, attendance, and eligibility for rehire and personal comments.

Communicating the Decision

The method of communicating the decision is important whether it involves offering a position to the successful candidate or rejecting an applicant.

ACCEPTING THE APPLICANT. An employment offer should confirm the terms of employment: the job, the hours and scheduling, probationary period, start date, and so on. The offer can be made either verbally or in writing. Even if the offer is made verbally, it is often good practice to send a confirming letter. Such an approach not only is courteous but also prevents future misunderstandings.

REJECTING THE APPLICANT. The groundwork for possible rejection should be laid early in the interviewing process. An applicant should never be led on. If there is a question about suitability for a position, the simple explanation should be made that other applicants will be seen and that acceptance will depend on a number of factors including the competition.

In rejecting an applicant it is best to give an objective, specific, and truthful but tactful reason. The reason should be tied to a lack of skills or to information provided by the applicant in the interview—a need for more bookkeeping knowledge or faster typing, stated unavailability for overtime or weekend shifts, a long history of absenteeism, a dislike for working with the elderly or the young, or on figures or at a desk job, or the like.

When there has been extensive interviewing for a key position or there is a possibly sensitive situation, it is a good practice to send a letter of rejection which makes it clear that the applicant was considered, that he has many fine qualifications, but that the decision favored an individual with even stronger credentials.

TURNOVER

People no longer continue to live in the community in which they were born and grew up. Neither is it ordinary for individuals to spend their entire employment span working for one organization. Even among top management, this is the era of geographic and social mobility, of job swapping, ladder climbing, and the head-hunter. At the same time, staff turnover can cost thousands and tens of thousands of dollars in recruiting, training, and the loss of production during the training or orientation period. Even though some turnover is inevitable, it is important to avoid preventable turnover. Since turnover control requires an analysis of where and why turnover exists, statistical data must be collected and put into a form that will uncover meaningful trends and patterns, in other words, a turnover report. Then the causes of the trends must be investigated with an eye to solving the problems leading to turnover.

The Turnover Report

The periodic turnover report, the vehicle most frequently used to obtain meaningful statistics, records turnover as a ratio of terminations to the number of people in the workforce for the organization as a whole and for specified groups within the organization. The format and details of the report can vary depending on several things: the size of the operation, management style, and the orientation of those who will use the report. It should start with a compilation of statistics and then be refined into a summary of information to be used as a management tool.

Although turnover reports are often regarded as necessary only in the larger organizations, they should not be neglected in smaller ones. Even simple and informal notations in a notebook will provide some telling statistics that will more than justify the time investment.

ESTABLISHING STATISTICS. Regardless of format or formality, certain elemental information is basic:

1. Number of terminations. This can be broken down by sec-

tion, division, department, job category, salary class, or in whatever terms are meaningful to the situation—accounting, data processing, public relations, legal, or client services; clerical, professional, technical, or service worker; under $8,000, $8,000 to $12,000, or $12,000 to $18,000; and so on.

2. Reasons for termination. A number of categories cover this topic: termination for cause (fired), more money, advancement, relocation, retirement, change of occupation, dissatisfaction, layoff, or abandonment. It may be easier to work with codes such as 1—termination for cause and 2—more money.

3. Length of service. This will help spotlight special-problem areas including employee morale, supervisory weaknesses, and employee reactions to changes in work patterns. Again, convenience may dictate the use of groups and codes—under 3 months, 3 to 6 months, 6 to 12 months, and so on.

4. Percents. Percents should be calculated to reflect turnover for the entire organization and for the categories selected for the report.

Percents are calculated by dividing the number of separations by the average number of the workforce for the period and multiplying by 100. For instance:

10 separations ÷ 75 workers × 100 = 13.3 percent.

Percents for items 2 and 3 are calculated by dividing the number of separations for the period by the total number of separations and multiplying by 100:

3 terminations ÷ 14 separations × 100 = 21.4 percent.

5. Number of new hires (optional). This should be broken down into the same categories as in item 1.

6. Sources of new hires (optional). Once again it may be practical to use codes: 1—employee referral, 2—private agency, 3—public agency, 4—advertising, and so on.

COLLECTING DATA. Numbers and statistics can be the concern of a clerical worker or can be tallied by a computer.

SOURCES OF INFORMATION. The numbers are a matter of counting. Special attention should be given to establishing and evaluating the personal sources of information that go beyond numbers—letters of resignation, transmittal notices from supervisors, termination questionnaires, and exit interviews.

Often it is a good idea to route terminating employees through the personnel function to confirm mailing addresses, assure the return of keys, uniforms, company identification, and the like, and to offer insurance conversion options. In larger organizations it may be useful and interesting to have employees complete termination questionnaires. Exit interviews, even if they are conducted on an informal basis, also are good sources of information.

The questionnaires should include standard questions such as reason for leaving, whether the job was well explained during the interview process, whether the employee enjoyed his employment and why, inquiries about benefits, strengths and weaknesses of his supervisor, and similar items. No name or signature should be requested; it is important to stress that the information is confidential and will not be recorded, included in the employee's record, or discussed with his supervisor.

Exit interviews also should be off the record. In the formal interview situation that fact should be stressed to the employee. The expressed purpose of the interview should be to learn the employee's general opinions of the working environment, benefits, holidays, and comparable experiences. Specific questions geared to the situation can follow—supervisory competence, co-workers, whether he has another job lined up, why he considers the new position to be better, what he'd like to see changed, and so forth. *Notes should not be taken* in the employee's presence unless they concern objective topics like benefits and holidays; any such notes should be explained to the employee. It is essential to preserve the interview as confidential and off the record. If the employee thinks that his remarks will affect his record or reference, he will not be candid and the data will not be worthwhile. In addition, the data must be interpreted as information from subjective sources. Both supervisors and terminating employees may color their answers, whether deliberately or subconsciously.

Questionnaires can often be used routinely. Exit interviews are excellent when there is the time and/or staff to handle them on a routine basis. If that is not possible, they can be conducted on a random basis or when there is a problem or trend that merits attention.

DEVELOPING THE DATA. The basic information listed above

should be taken a step further and developed so that it can provide a picture of trends. Statistics can be summarized, divided, and subdivided to produce complex webs of details, combinations, and cross sections, all of which can be fascinating. But it is important to pare the report down to the information that will be used. Depending on organizational needs and the structure into which the data are placed, there are a number of topics that can be incorporated in the report:

1. Departmental, divisional, and/or sectional numbers and percents.
2. Occupational numbers and percents.
3. Monthly, quarterly, and year-to-date figures.
4. Breakdown of terminations, in numbers and percents, with respect to length of service, occupation, reasons for leaving, and so on.
5. Comparison of occupational statistics between departments.
6. Summaries of reasons for leaving, according to department, length of service, occupation, and so on.
7. Comparison with previous experiences.

The combinations and possibilities are there to be developed and used according to need.

ANALYZING THE DATA. The data so collected and refined should be used to determine whether patterns and trends are forming. Problem areas can be identified by looking at the following checkpoints.

1. Divisional, departmental, or sectional statistics. Is there one department with a consistently higher percent of turnover? If so, is there a common reason for the separations?
2. Compensation. Is there a high percent of turnover in the organization as a whole or among an occupational group who leave for more money?
3. Short-term employment. Is there a pattern of employees leaving after a short term? Is it particularly prevalent among those working in a given area?
4. Advancement. Are a significant number of employees able to find better jobs—with other employers?
5. Minority problems. Is there high turnover among females

or other minorities? Is it prevalent throughout the organization or limited to specific departments or supervisors?
6. Disciplinary terminations. Is there a consistently high percent of abandonments or terminations for cause?

In addition to monthly turnover reports, it may be helpful to prepare quarterly, semiannual, or annual reports which combine statistics. A narrative analysis in which the potential problems are discussed and are proved or dispelled may be included.

Preventing Turnover

The best way to avoid turnover is to hire able and interested people and keep them happy. In other words, worker stability is more likely to be achieved by or with good selection and placement techniques, adequate compensation, orientation and training programs, well-trained supervisors, and a generally positive employee-management relationship. But even the best-designed personnel program must be monitored and kept up to date. The turnover report can be as good a tool in personnel management as the profit-and-loss statement is in financial management.

WAGES. A significant number of resignations for "more money" may indicate a companywide problem or represent a special situation for a particular occupational group. A review of job descriptions and evaluations and salary survey may be in order. If necessary, consideration should be given to adjusting the wage scale or reevaluating individual jobs. If a specific occupational group is involved, it may be necessary to red-circle the job(s) in question (see Chapter 3).

SUPERVISION. Criticism of supervisors should be analyzed with care. Employees may be reacting against new procedures, changes in the work routine, justified discipline, a new supervisor, or similar circumstances. But repeated complaints concerning the same supervisor deserve attention. An informal chat with the supervisor about the turnover, not the criticism, may explain the problem. Or perhaps a discussion with the supervisor's superior will alert him to the need to give guidance or counseling to the supervisor. It may be that formal training is needed (see Chapter 7). If the problem is serious, disciplinary measures, including termination of the supervisor, may be in the organization's interest.

LACK OF ADVANCEMENT. If outsiders are brought into higher positions within the organization without considering current staff, management may well be passing over or failing to recognize in-house talent. If it is necessary to fill higher-ranking jobs from outside sources, the reasons should be communicated to employees. This can be done indirectly by circulating a description of the new person's credentials (organizing an announcement memo or newsletter item will accomplish it). In isolated instances it may be advisable to have a conference with an employee who might have expected such a promotion to explain that he was considered. He should be told why someone else was hired and be assured that he'll be considered for future advancement. If there is no room for promotion, jobs might be "enriched"; that is, additional responsibilities might be delegated to an individual to provide a more stimulating and efficient job situation.

MINORITY PROBLEMS. Consistently high turnover among minorities and women may point to inefficient personnel utilizations, failure to provide appropriate advancement, or a supervisor-related problem.

SHORT-TERM EMPLOYMENT. Quick turnover may relate to poor selection criteria, a poor supervisory practice, or lack of orientation and training. If under- or overqualified applicants are hired consistently, the cause should be traced; it may be supervisory preference, poor referrals, inadequate job descriptions and specifications, or faulty communications. If one supervisor or department is involved, supervisory practices should be studied.

DISCIPLINE. A disproportionate number of discipline-related terminations may reflect a need to revise rules, regulations, or disciplinary procedures. Additional supervisory training or more counseling to supervisors and employees may be necessary. It may be a matter of improving communications so that employees will understand rules and call-in procedures more clearly.

Whatever areas are considered, the thrust of such a program should be to uncover problems and seek solutions even if radical action is required.

3 WAGE-AND-SALARY ADMINISTRATION

To the employer the payment of wages and salaries is a substantial expenditure. To the employee the monies he earns represent not only his livelihood but a tangible recognition of his worth to the organization. For both parties, therefore, it is important to have a rational and objective basis for decisions affecting individual compensation both as part of the initial terms of employment and as an ongoing process. Thus the purpose of a wage-and-salary program is the formulation of a wage structure for the entire organization and the establishment of policies for administering the plan.

THE WAGE STRUCTURE

In effect, a wage structure creates within the organization a hierarchy in which jobs are priced to reflect content, demands, and levels of responsibility; it also establishes pay rates that are competitive within the geographic area. Thus, on the one hand, a corporation president will be paid more than a vice president, and managers and professional employees will be paid more than clerical workers; on the other hand, the compensation for each of those positions will be competitive with salaries and wages paid for positions of similar responsibility in comparable organizations.

Although each organization, depending on size and complexity, has unique needs that must be met by its wage-and-salary program, the components and principles are constant. Jobs first must be defined and described and then evaluated relative to one another; a wage scale must be devised to reflect organization resources and goals; and a system for calculating increments must be devised.

The Job Description

The job description is the foundation of the wage-and-salary program since it provides the basic data for job comparison and evaluation. Its importance in justifying wage determinations has been proved by daily application in scores of corporations and has been reinforced by recent suits under the Equal Pay Act in which court rulings were based on job descriptions and evaluations. Daily usage and legal proceedings underscore completeness of information as the key to internal utility and value as evidence.

CONTENTS. The format and formality of job descriptions can vary considerably. Indeed, it is not uncommon to use two formats within the same organization: a task-oriented job description for support personnel and a narrative type that emphasizes the level of responsibility and accountability of the function for executives and managers. Whatever the format, it should present a comprehensive picture of the job including the tasks and activities, the parameters of responsibility, and the circumstances in which the job is performed. A breakdown of suitable information would include the following.

1. Duties. There should be a complete list of the tasks and assignments, including information concerning complexity, degree of difficulty, frequency, and importance. The job description for an accounting clerk, for example, might include the following statement: "daily totals cash received, makes entries in accounts receivable logbook, and posts payments on client records for 45 or more ongoing accounts representing $25,000 in monthly income." Tasks performed only occasionally or in relief of other functions should be included with appropriate differentiation. Formal job descriptions should include a statement that provides management with some flexibility in work assignments such as "performs other related duties as required" or "duties include but are not limited to. . . ."

2. Supervision received. Both the nature and source of supervision should be identified. Supervision may be direct or general, or work may be performed under the "direction" of a superior. Direct supervision generally is received by the lower-

level employee whose work and on-the-job behavior are observed or checked closely, for example, file clerk, typist, or production worker. General supervision usually is given to a higher-level job—secretary, nurse, and some lower-level supervisors. Direction indicates that work is performed independently and results and progress are measured by a superior who provides guidance and insures production; an assistant department head works under the direction of the department head, who in turn may work under the direction of a member of higher management. The source of supervision should be stated in terms of the position(s) from which supervision is received. In most cases the immediate superior will provide supervision, but sometimes an employee or some aspects of his work can be guided or overseen by a professional, "lead," or senior employee who assists the direct superior.

3. Supervision given. Any supervisory responsibilities, full- or part-time, and the nature of that supervision should be defined in accordance with the distinctions defined above. The occupations receiving the supervision should be mentioned, and in some cases the numbers of employees supervised should be indicated.

4. Special requirements. The skills, physical demands, education, experience, and miscellaneous requirements for the job are an important part of the job description. (See Chapter 9 regarding governmental regulations and EEOC guidelines.) They may include physical demands or hazards such as heavy lifting, use of mechanical or electrical equipment, or working at heights or statements regarding the pace, pressure, need for independent action, and working environment. Special skills and educational requirements should be specified—communication skills, speed of secretarial skills, degree, and so on.

5. Approval or reviews. Individuals with authority and knowledge of the job and/or the job description process—department head, administrator, and personnel director—should be asked to review and approve the content of each job description. Their comments and approval should be made part of a permanent backup record.

Although the job description should provide a comprehensive and complete view of the job and its requirements, it should be written concisely and include little discussion. It is intended as a broad outline. Work schedules, procedure manuals, methodology, and protocols have different purposes and should not be incorporated. Such inclusions at once detract from the job description and are inadequate to meet other needs. Even job descriptions with narrative formats should be limited to relevant materials and should avoid extraneous issues.

The best source of information about each job is usually the person who does it daily. The employee can be asked to complete a simple job questionnaire (Figures 11 and 12) that asks for the information required in the above categories. If possible, the job description writer should interview the employee, observe working conditions, acquaint himself with the complexities of the job and/or the equipment used, and in general develop an awareness of the job as a whole. Sometimes it is also a good idea to interview the supervisor. In all cases, the supervisor should be shown a draft of the job description and be asked to check for accuracy and completeness.

USAGE. Although the job description is intended primarily to provide a foundation for wage-and-salary programs, it can be useful in several other areas. By providing a clear and concise outline of functions, it can be a tool in organizing departments and structuring reporting relations. In recruiting, the job descriptions provide the interviewer with comprehensive information regarding the vacancy and job requirements; in some instances they can be given to a serious candidate for employment so that he can form a judgment regarding his interest in and suitability for the position.

When employees are being evaluated, the job description is an objective statement of responsibilities to be used as a standard of comparison and to establish a mutual understanding of duties, parameters, and need for improvement. For the trainer it provides a frame of reference and a checklist to insure thoroughness and accuracy. Within some fields job descriptions form the basis of legal restraints and liabilities.

Job Evaluation

Job evaluation is a method of comparing jobs on the basis of objective criteria to establish their relative value within the organization. Since the focus of the evaluation process is on job design within the organizational structure, jobs are measured

Figure II. Job questionnaire for exempt personnel.

Name_____

Job Title_____ Department _____ How Long on Job _____

Give brief statement describing your responsibilities including fiscal management and responsibility for work direction of others. Specify dollar values and titles where appropriate, indicate areas of major involvement.

(continue on reverse side if necessary)

To whom are you accountable (title, not name)?

Do you consider your job to require

- [ ] General management ability
- [ ] High level of technical expertise
- [ ] Creativity

- [ ] Interpersonal skills
- [ ] Ability to function under pressure
- [ ] Fiscal management skills

What educational prerequisites are necessary to do your job?_____

_____

What experience is required?_____

_____

What personal characteristics are needed? _____

_____

Employee Signature _____ Date _____

Figure 12. Job questionnaire for support personnel.

Employee Name _____

Job Title _____ Department _____ Start Date _____

In order of importance list the duties of your job. Use clear precise words; avoid vague words like "handle" and "process."

(continue on reverse side if necessary)

List the kinds of equipment you use in performing your job (typewriter, adding machine, copier, keypunch, etc.).

Check the appropriate boxes to indicate the skills required in your job. Omit your own qualifications unless they are required by the job.

- ☐ Typing – speed _____
- ☐ Shorthand – speed ____
- ☐ Bookkeeping
- ☐ Filing
- ☐ Dictating Machine
- ☐ Storekeeping

- ☐ Simple mathematical calculations. (addition, subtraction, multiplication, division)
- ☐ Semicomplex mathematical computations. (Fractions, %, rates)
- ☐ Other (specify) _____

What educational level is required by the job?   0-8 yrs. ☐

10 yrs. ☐   12 yrs. ☐   14 yrs. ☐   16 yrs. ☐   other ☐

Any specific courses (specify) _____

What experience level is required by the job?

0-1 yr. ☐   1-2 yrs. ☐   2-5 yrs. ☐

What is your educational background? _____

What was your previous experience? _____

Do you feel you were qualified ☐   underqualified ☐

overqualified ☐   for the position when hired?

Would you benefit from additional training?   Yes ☐   No ☐

Employee Signature _____ Date _____

against common standards and are ranked accordingly. Although the standards will vary to reflect the nature and needs of the organization, the objective is always to establish a hierarchy in which the more demanding occupations are rated higher so that job requirements can be correlated with salary.

In order to insure equity, there should be well-defined standards and delineations. By way of example, one category commonly used in the evaluating process is the amount of supervision required by the function under normal circumstances. Five levels of "supervision received" can be described:

1. Close or direct supervision is normally required or work is of such routine nature that limitations and procedures are clear.
2. Close supervision is frequently required.
3. Supervision is moderately close, but some direct supervision is needed.
4. General supervision is maintained primarily through periodic conferences, reports, inspections, and results.
5. Little if any supervision is required beyond periodic consultation and reports. Emphasis is on results.

When executive or management positions are evaluated, the standards might center around the amount and kind of impact on budget, accountability, and similar factors.

Simplistically speaking, there are two basic methods of evaluating jobs: the factor system and slotting. Whichever is used, the key is to define standards and measurements as described above and apply them only to *jobs*. At this point function and incumbent should be divorced. Individual performance evaluation is a separate process which will be discussed subsequently in this chapter.

THE FACTOR SYSTEM. The factor system is a complex and formalized rating system with many variations. Generally speaking, each job is rated against established categories, or factors, such as "supervision received." Within that factor specific numbers of points are assigned to various levels in ascending order. In the case of supervision received, "close supervision" may be allocated 3 points and "little supervision" 12 points. In some cases the factors are weighted to reflect importance in much the same way that certain dives or gymnastic movements are assigned "degrees of difficulty" in competitive scoring. When the points are totaled for all jobs, there will be a mathematical ranking of jobs with the more-demanding positions receiving a higher number of points. Jobs within a reasonable range of points will be assigned the same salary grades or placed in the same salary categories.

There are a number of sources to consult for establishing a factor system; they include government systems, private consultants, trade associations, and employer groups. Alternatively, a rather simple mathematical formula can be put together on an individual basis. Some systems lend themselves more naturally to executive positions, and others seem more suitable for nonmanagement jobs. Just as different formats can be used for management and nonmanagement job descriptions, so it may be advantageous to develop different factors to evaluate those job categories.

SLOTTING. Slotting is a less-formalized method of evaluating jobs. Each position is reviewed and assigned a rank. Although no mathematical formula is involved, standards and definitions should be developed to insure objectivity. To rank jobs, it is best to select key positions as landmarks. The least and most demanding positions in the organization or group may be selected first and other jobs compared to them. In evaluating support positions, for instance, a file clerk clearly may be in the lowest rank and a typist in the next higher rank, followed by a secretary, bookkeeper, and executive secretary. The slotting method is the easiest and most reasonable for the small organization and in organizations in which distinctions are easily discernible. When dissimilar functions must be evaluated and assimilated into the same salary structure, a factor system is usually more suitable.

The Salary Scale

The salary scale is constructed by compiling the data from the evaluating process and current salary practices, grouping jobs into logical categories or grades, and establishing salary ranges and pay policies based on community practices, affordability, and company goals.

ESTABLISHING SALARY GROUPS. The first step in setting up salary groups or grades is to list in columns all the jobs in the organization from the lowest-ranked job (or that with the lowest number of points) to the highest. If the factor system has been used, a reasonable point spread should be used to define categories and columns should be added to indicate point groups and assigned points. If jobs have been ranked by slotting, jobs close in ranking should be slotted into the same category. Other columns should include the current starting salary for each job and the starting range of competitive employers in the community. The resulting composite of information will be similar to the mythical data in Table 1.

Table 1. Examples of salary groups.

POINT SPREAD	JOB TITLE	ASSIGNED POINTS	CURRENT STARTS	SALARY STARTS
0–150	File clerk	143	3.03	3.09–3.49
	Messenger	148	3.10	3.08–3.55
151–175	Clerk typist	165	3.23	3.05–3.50
	Senior mail clerk	171	3.20	3.15–3.42
176–200	Accounting clerk	180	3.35	3.20–3.60
	Junior secretary	178	3.43	3.25–3.70
201–225	Payroll clerk	220	3.45	3.30–3.75
226–250	Secretary	229	3.60	3.39–3.85
251–275				
276–300	Senior payroll clerk	283	3.75	3.85–4.00
301–325				
326–350	Senior secretary	343	4.17	4.15–4.27

The groups in the table could be assigned grades in keeping with the point spreads shown. Thus, a point spread of 0–150 would be Grade I, 151–175 would be Grade II, and so forth through Grade IX. Although no jobs have fallen into the point spread for Grades VI and VIII, those grades would be available for future expansion.

Competitive wage information can be obtained through a salary survey of similar organizations in the community. The survey can be conducted by phone or mail. In either case it is advisable to include with the job title a one- or two-sentence job description to insure that functions as well as titles are similar. Employers often are willing to share such information and exchange copies of survey results.

Although similar information is available on a geographical basis from Bureau of Labor Statistics surveys, the lag time in compiling the data usually results in the publication of outdated information which requires cost-of-living or similar adjustment. Trade or employer associations or local chambers of commerce may have more recent data. Whatever the source, pay rates will vary tremendously according to the geographic area and reflect community custom, cost-of-living variances, and in some cases the extent of industrialization in the area.

SALARY RANGES. Once the basic data have been compiled and collated, starting salaries and salary ranges must be established. At this point a basic decision regarding salary goals must be made. Most employers opt for salaries in the "average" range. However, a desire to attract top employees, a shortage of labor, an effort to avoid unionization, competition with union shops, or similar circumstances may make a relatively high salary scale advisable. On the other hand, an unusual benefit or labor situation may allow salaries to be set in the lower range of community standards.

Unless management has decided to increase salary levels, most jobs will probably remain in about the same range. In some cases the new salary structure will establish slightly higher starting rates and in others slightly lower ones. Again, since the focus at this point is on structure and *new* starting rates, the effect of the new rates on current employees should be disregarded. That problem must be handled as a separate issue and will be discussed in that context.

Establishing starting salaries requires the manipulation of figures and percents in the context of the data compiled above until a workable structure evolves. Generally it is easier to start with jobs for which salary needs are clear—usually the lower-ranked positions. In industries in which certain jobs commonly receive the minimum wage, Grade I will be set at that level or however much higher the individual employer chooses.

The data in Table 1 indicate that the company's current rate for a file clerk is low in the community but the starting rate for a messenger is competitive. Setting the file clerk rate at the same level as the messenger, rated just five points higher, would establish an equitable rate within the company and give the organization a comfortable position within the marketplace for both jobs. The next step is to find a logical pattern for figures for the ascending grades, again by playing with figures until the formula is derived to provide uniform distinction or logical patterns of differentiation while accommodating the salary requirements of the jobs. Grade assignments and percentages should be tested and adjusted until an appropriate scale emerges. In Table 2 a 4 percent differential is sufficient to place salaries in the range consistent with the data of Table 1.

Table 2. Examples of salary range.

GRADE	JOB TITLE	NEW START
I	File clerk, messenger	$3.10
II	Clerk typist, senior mail clerk	3.22
III	Accounting clerk, junior secretary	3.35
IV	Payroll clerk	3.48
V	Secretary	3.62
VI	—	3.76
VII	Senior payroll clerk	3.91
VIII	—	4.06
IX	Senior secretary	4.22
X *	—	4.39

* Grade X has been added to round out the number of grades and to allow for expansion.

A salary range must be established that will allow for salary increases for the individual but, at the same time, recognize that there is a limit to the dollar value of each job. Again, the range will reflect the particular organization, community custom, and system of raises. It should be broad enough to encourage longevity and prevent too much internal compression. A range of 30 to 35 percent would provide about five years' worth of raises for the average employee who receives a 5 percent merit raise annually. There are a number of methods for determining wage increases. The selection of any one system should be based on the amount of budgetary flexibility the organization can absorb and the character of the supervisory staff.

Salaries can be increased by a percentage determined by the performance review, which will be discussed later in this chapter. The method is simple and provides greater flexibility, but, depending on the supervisory staff, it is sometimes more difficult to administer, budget, and control. To maintain equity, it is necessary to insure common understanding of performance standards and to monitor carefully the correlation between standards and the percent of increase.

Within the percentage method there are many variations. A midpoint that employees are expected to reach after a certain length of time can be established. In some organizations salaries are advanced more quickly before the midpoint is reached and at a slower rate thereafter. That system does get the employee advanced into a higher salary more quickly than most and might make job changing financially disadvantageous. However, it decreases incentives for employees with longer service.

Another method involves setting up an exact salary scale with prescribed steps:

GRADE	A	B	C	D	E	F	G
I	3.10	3.20	3.42	3.59	3.77	3.96	4.12
II	3.22	3.38	3.55	3.73	3.92	4.12	4.33

An employee with a satisfactory performance review would receive a one-step increase, for example, from $3.10 to $3.20. In rare instances, with special approval, a two-step increase might be given to an outstanding employee. The system is very easy to administer and control, and it can therefore be more effective in larger organizations and those with less sophisticated supervisors.

In many instances the step method of determining increases is used for support or nonexempt personnel and the percentage method for managers and professionals.

EXCEPTIONS. When job evaluation results are correlated with current and community pay scales, it is not unusual to discover that certain occupations have been paid at rates disproportionate to (usually higher than) their evaluations. That is apt to occur when labor is in short supply, certain skills are in great demand, and the occupations in demand tend to be unionized within the geographic area. When that situation occurs, the evaluation should be rechecked to insure that the factors have been rated accurately. If a corrected, not manipulated, evaluation does not put the job into a realistic salary range, it is necessary to regrade the job to the appropriate level despite the discrepancy. The process of regrading the job to meet the external dollar value is known as red-circling. If too many jobs need to be red-circled, there may be a flaw in the evaluation process.

The other exception may be the individual who is being paid out of scale. First it is important to insure that the employee is in fact doing the job described and not a higher-level job with a lower title. If the employee is titled correctly, he should be red-circled and his wages frozen so that he will not be eligible for merit increases until his pay is in line with the evaluated rate. If his performance is good, that might be reason to consider adding to his responsibilities and/or skills to justify the wage rate. If promotional opportunities are available, the employee may be a likely candidate for advancement.

Costing and Installing the New Wage Plan

A new wage plan can be installed in either of two basic ways: (1) immediate installation, in which the salaries of all employees are adjusted at one time, or (2) a more gradual approach, in which salaries are adjusted as performance review dates are reached. The latter method will be cheaper but can take almost a year to complete. Of course, a variation also can be worked out: those whose performance review dates will come up in the next three or six months can receive immediate adjustments; in three or six months the wages of those whose review dates will come up in the next period will be adjusted; and so on. The decision to implement the new plan immediately or gradually will depend on the individual situation: the availability of labor, employee pressure, union activity in the community (see Chapter 10 for restrictions), and cost.

COSTING THE PLAN. Regardless of the implementation schedule preferred, it is advisable to estimate the plan's cost and its impact on individual employees before announcing its implementation to the workforce. That involves calculating the difference in basic wages under the old and new systems, including the expected increments to be awarded at performance review dates. If a significant amount of overtime is anticipated, that cost should be added.

INSTALLATION. Before wages are adjusted, supervisors should review the performance of each employee. Based on performance, longevity, method of implementation, and next review date, each employee should be assigned a confirmed place in the salary scale. Although longevity should be a factor, employees should not be assigned automatically to the highest part of the new salary range. Care must be taken to correct rather than perpetuate old inequities, but judgment must be exercised. In most cases employees will fit into a place in the scale nearest their current salaries. If current salaries are higher, those employees can be frozen at their current rates until their review dates. If possible, employees should not be placed at the top of the salary range, since no room would be left for future increments.

When the new rates have been determined, each employee should be called in for a conference. The new system and the worker's place in it should be explained, and the employee's performance review should be discussed. Some employees may receive merit increases and be put into the salary scale simultaneously. Others may get adjustments that should not be passed off as raises, since the difference may be as small as one to three cents per hour. In such instances it is imperative to explain to the employees that their salaries are not being raised but only adjusted to get them into the new system. The employees should be told when they will be eligible for merit increases. In cases of clearly substandard performance, adjustments may be withheld. In such instances a definite date for a new review should be scheduled in accordance with the performance review procedures discussed below.

ADMINISTERING THE PLAN

The wage-and-salary scale provides a system for assigning dollar values to jobs. The other half of wage-and-salary administration involves compensating the individual within that scale. That includes establishing initial salaries for new employees and providing a method of recognizing meritorious service with financial remuneration. Three points should be stressed.

First, it is essential to have hard-and-fast rules for salary administration and to apply those rules universally. Exceptions will create dissatisfaction among employees that at best will be detrimental to morale and turnover and at worst will lead to union leanings and/or charges of discrimination. No matter how confidential salary information is regarded by management, no matter what safeguards are established for record security, individuals always will discuss their own salaries and raises and will relay any information they possess concerning the salaries and raises of their associates. The solution is to establish a set of guidelines, insure that the guidelines are nondiscriminatory, see that the guidelines are followed without exception, and explain the nature of the wage program to employees.

Second, raises should not be the sole method of providing motivation. Although the absence of a system for reviewing salaries will destroy motivation, financial concerns are only one motivating factor. (See Chapter 6, Motivation.)

Third, raises should be based on merit and should be given solely on the basis of satisfactory performance. Cost-of-living adjustments should be handled separately. If such an adjustment is deemed advisable, the entire wage scale should be adjusted to reflect the change and should be extended to all employees regardless of merit and red-circling. It is important to communicate to employees that there is a difference between merit increases and cost-of-living adjustments and to gain as much employee relations mileage as possible whenever the salary scale is upgraded to reflect the latter.

Establishing the Initial Salary

The salary range established for each job should have as its minimum the rate needed to compensate an individual whose background and experience indicate that he has the ability to perform the functions of the job at a satisfactory level with a normal amount of orientation. There are two other categories of potential employees: the trainee and the candidate with higher qualifications.

THE TRAINEE. When people are hired for formal training programs or on the condition that they acquire a specified skill essential to the job, they may start at a lower rate, such as 95 percent of the usual rate, as long as that amount is above the minimum wage. Wages can be increased as soon as the training is completed or the skill is acquired. A hospital or nursing home, for instance, might hire individuals with no prior nursing experience and conduct a six-week training course; such personnel would be hired at 95 percent of the usual rate and raised to the usual wage at the end of the six weeks. A secretary whose shorthand is rusty might be employed on the condition that a brush-up course be taken; at the end of the course or when a speed test is passed, that person's salary could be adjusted from 95 percent to the beginning rate for the job.

THE MORE QUALIFIED CANDIDATE. A candidate with a level of training or experience high enough to insure better than average performance with a minimum of orientation might start at a salary 5 percent higher than that position's normal starting rate. An accountant or nurse with an advanced degree and/or two years of experience might rate such a wage. Definite guidelines should be drawn up to monitor advanced starting rates to avoid discrimination, favoritism, and the erosion of the system.

Wage Increments

Raises are important to employees not only because of the monetary implications but also because wage increments represent concrete evidence of work progress, supervisory opinion, and treatment as compared with that of fellow workers. The implications of uneven administration of salary increases are such that attention must be paid to the scheduling of wage increments, performance criteria and review systems, performance review communications, and the amounts of raises.

SCHEDULING. Performance reviews and projected wage increases should be scheduled at regular and logical intervals. The end of the probationary period should be an occasion for the first formal performance review, since it will force the supervisor to decide whether an employee is satisfactory and should be retained or is unsatisfactory and subject to termination. A review at that time will provide successful employees with early evidence of interest in his development and proof that good performance will be rewarded financially. In addition, terminating unsatisfactory employees as soon as poor performance can be identified not only will help to improve overall efficiency, production, and morale but will also reduce costs of training, benefits, and unemployment compensation.

Additional reviews should be scheduled at prescribed intervals such as the anniversary of employment. A monitoring system should be set up so that reviews are scheduled, completed, and processed in timely fashion. In larger organizations, the person responsible for the personnel function should initiate the process by distributing performance review forms far enough in advance to permit thoughtful reviews and timely processing of wage adjustments. Supervisors should be accountable for prompt completion of the review forms and discussion with employees.

THE PERFORMANCE REVIEW. The most obvious part of the performance review is the rating of the employee by his supervisor. Even in a small office where personnel programs are less structured and formal, it is necessary to devise a standardized format, define performance standards, and make sure that all supervisors have a common understanding of the factors and standards.

A performance review form should reflect the goals of the organization. The traits to be evaluated should be specific, understandable by all raters in the same way, applicable to all those who will be evaluated, and observable by supervisors on a daily basis. Some "old reliables" include quality and quantity of work, initiative, judgment, dependability, leadership, creativeness, adaptability, grooming, and the ability to work with others. Whichever factors are selected, a system of factors should be established and the degrees defined:

Ability to work with others
Poor—unfriendly and reluctant to deal with others; indifferent
Acceptable—does what is necessary; accepted by others but lacks interest in working with them
Good—cooperates well; gets along with co-workers and outside contacts; good team person
Outstanding—goes out of way to get along with and work with other employees and outsiders; has high acceptance by both

Whatever factors are selected for performance review should lend themselves to objective measurement as indicated above. Criteria such as "attitude" stress personality rather than performance and deal with immeasurable issues.

Just as there is no one set of factors appropriate for all situations, so there is no magic format. However, there are some basic principles to be kept in mind. The format should require supervisors to think and to be specific. Words such as "good," "fair,"

and "poor" leave much room for subjectivity. It is better to devise a system so that supervisors can assign a specific numerical
• value to performance. The form should include room for supervisors to back up their judgments with specific statements concerning the employee's performance. The numerical values assigned to each factor could be averaged to give an overall performance rating.

Quality of work

POOR	FAIR	AVERAGE	GOOD	EXCELLENT
0 1.0	1.5 2.0	2.5 3.0	3.5 4.0	4.5 5.0

Usually completes assignments accurately but errors are not uncommon and employee does not always check his own work before turning it in.
Points = 3.0

The performance review form should also provide spaces in which the supervisor can suggest steps the employee can take to improve his own performance and ways the supervisor can assist him. Room should be provided for the employee to comment in writing about the review, and there should be spaces for the signature of the employee, supervisor, and department head and the date.

The performance review form should be completed by the immediate supervisor, but individuals who contribute to supervising the employee—a lead person, professional, or an assistant who provides work direction—should be asked for input. The amount of such input will vary with the supervisor's position; and when input is significant, a separate statement might be in order. The department head should review the evaluation before the performance review interview with the employee.

Because of the difference in accountability and responsibility of the two groups, it is often advantageous to develop two different forms: one for management and professional employees and the other for support personnel. The form for the management group will emphasize accountability, responsibility, and potential rather than such factors as quantity and quality of work that are traditionally emphasized in evaluating nonmanagement personnel.

THE EVALUATION INTERVIEW. The second part of the performance review is the interview that spotlights both the supervisor and the employee. On the one hand, the supervisor is forced to make certain judgments about the employee's performance and value and then discuss and justify those conclusions with objectivity. On the other hand, the employee must face a thorough critique and an airing of his shortcomings. Being aware of the employee's reactions to the situation (after all, his performance is reviewed too), the supervisor can become too hesitant and less forthright than necessary to achieve the desired effect. Nonetheless, the performance review is the key to both the administration of the wage-and-salary program and effective supervision.

Good supervision requires giving employees daily feedback regarding performance. (See Chapter 7.) Since it is a formalized extension of the day-to-day supervisor-employee relationship, the performance review should contain no surprises, no hoarded criticisms, no new information. Its value is threefold: it forces the supervisor to be comprehensive in his estimation of the employee, to look for performance patterns, and to seek means of developing the employee; it provides feedback to the employee about both good and bad; it establishes clearly in the employee's mind the connection between good performance and financial reward.

There is, of course, no magic formula for conducting the performance review interview. The supervisor's style and the relationship between the supervisor and the employee will be the determining factors. However, there are some basic rules which should be followed.

1. Establishing the atmosphere. The interview must be conducted in privacy where both participants will be physically and psychologically comfortable. There should be no interruptions, and sufficient time should be budgeted so that the review will be thorough and questions and problems can be discussed.

2. Putting the employee at ease. The employee must be assured that the process is not meant to be a fault-finding session or a "roast" but is an opportunity for him to get comprehensive feedback about performance. He should be reminded that he has heard most of what will be brought up at different times throughout the period being reviewed.

3. Inviting the employee's participation. There are a number of techniques for fostering employee involvement in the evaluation interview. A more sophisticated employee might be asked to

rate himself either verbally as each factor is discussed or by completing a form; the employee might be given the review to read and then be asked for comments. Specific questions can be asked concerning the worker's reaction to specific ratings or about why he performs as he does, why he is late, why he does not check his own work, and so on.

4. Insuring a mutual understanding of the job and performance standards. If there is a written description of performance standards or a formal job description, it may be advisable to have the employee read it so that he has a clear understanding of performance criteria.

5. Specificity. It is important to be specific but not petty in comments and criticisms. When trends in performance are discussed, examples should be cited; instances that have been discussed previously are preferable.

6. Objectivity. Performance, not personality, and acts, not attitudes, should be the focus of the performance review. Personality and attitudes should be discussed only if they are directly and obviously related to performance, such as the manner of addressing clients, superiors, or co-workers.

7. Impersonality. The supervisor should not pry into the personal life of the employee. Personal problems should be discussed only if they are the cause of a performance problem, such as inattention to detail caused by preoccupation. Most likely a discussion of that kind will come about naturally if the supervisor asks the employee why he acts as he does.

8. Problem solving. The performance review presents a unique opportunity to show interest in the employee's development and provide assistance to help the employee succeed. If an employee is chronically late, for instance, because of a train schedule or unusual family situation, a slight adjustment in working hours may be a solution: lunch hours might be shortened, or starting and quitting times might be changed. Obviously such an adjustment is feasible only if it does not hamper operations and care is taken to prevent any hint of favoritism.

9. Changes in performance. Both improvements and areas of decline should be noted.

10. Performance improvement. Areas that need improvement should be identified and specific suggestions for achieving the improvements should be given. Poor spelling can be cor-

rected by using the dictionary; typing can be improved if 15 or 30 minutes is set aside each day for practice with an exercise book.

11. Potential. The employee's potential should be discussed, along with specific suggestions for reaching reasonable goals. A good accounting clerk might be encouraged to take accounting courses at night. Professional reading might be recommended for a professional to develop more perspective and job know-how.

12. Individuality. No comparisons should be made. The individual employee is to be evaluated against objective standards. Other people and their work should not be discussed.

13. Follow-up. Specific dates should be set up to discuss areas that need correction or development. The employee should be encouraged to return to the supervisor if he has questions or job-related problems. If necessary, definite times for coaching or counseling should be established.

14. Raise-performance correlations. The relation between the performance review and a potential increment should be explained. An increase should be withheld if poor performance warrants it, but such an action calls for another formal performance rating in 30, 60, or 90 days. The employee should be told exactly what improvements will have to be made if he is to merit a raise (or be retained) at that time.

15. Documentations. Any specific problems and suggestions that have been discussed and any follow-up dates that have been established should be documented.

16. Signature. The employee should sign the performance review even if he disagrees with it. If necessary, he should be assured that his signature does not denote agreement but only certifies that he has read the review. He should be invited to comment in writing even if he disagrees. If the employee wishes to contest a poor rating, he should be informed of his options—a written response to be included in his file, grievance procedure, or whatever. If the employee refuses to sign the form, another person should sign a statement that the employee refused to do so in his presence.

17. Positivism. If possible, the interview should end on a positive note. Of course, that is easy if the employee has a good

rating. If performance has been rated low, the positive note might be an expression of concern and encouragement.

18. Termination. Very poor performance is ground for termination. If the review marks the end of the probationary period either for a new employee or for a person previously put on probation for poor performance, termination should be immediate and linked directly to the review. If a poor rating is given to an employee with longer service and previously satisfactory ratings, counseling is in order, possibly to be followed by a probationary period and special review. That should be explained fully to the employee and documented in writing.

AMOUNTS. Increments will be on a step or percentage basis depending on what kind of program has been established. In either case, rules should be established and enforced uniformly. Step increases are probably the easiest form to administer. An employee with satisfactory to good ratings should get a one-step increase. The exceptional employee with a rating of excellent should be considered for a two-step increase. Before such a raise is discussed with the employee, it might be wise to obtain special approval from high authority within the organization.

Percent increases can be handled in several ways. A satisfactory to good rating might merit a certain percent of increase, for instance 5 percent, and an excellent rating might earn a higher increment such as 7 or 10 percent. Or, a gradation can be established—5 percent for satisfactory, 7 percent for good, and 10 percent for excellent.

When job descriptions and performance review systems stress accountability and results, particularly for management personnel, special care should be taken to dovetail increments with performance. In those instances, it is helpful to establish a point system for performance and to correlate point totals with percent of increases. It is not unusual to use a percent system for management personnel and a step system for nonmanagement employees.

4 BENEFITS

Although benefit programs usually are considered in terms of their impact on employees, the high cost to the employer of providing them—up to one-third of payroll expenditures—warrants a return on the employer's investment. Thus benefit programs should be developed not only to provide for the human needs and demands of the workforce but also to help develop the stability and morale that will improve production and stimulate income. That entails developing a program that will provide the desired coverage and at the same time maximize the employee relations value of the dollars spent.

Benefit programs, like wage-and-salary plans, are affected tremendously by community standards and/or industry custom. Since no employer can afford to fall too far behind his competitors in such areas and hope to attract qualified personnel, surveys should be made to find out what benefits others in the area are providing. However, the administration of the program can and should be designed to reflect the uniqueness of the organization, provide work incentives, and promote employee morale.

Benefits can be divided into three categories: time off (or leave), insured programs, and special benefits. Each category should be considered and decisions should be made on what benefits must be provided, what additional benefits *can* be offered, cost, and administration. Special emphasis should be placed on publicizing the program to inform employees about what is available as well as to demonstrate management's interest (and expenditures) in employee welfare.

TIME-OFF POLICIES

Paying employees for time not worked is a seeming incongruity in the economic structure. (Certainly Scrooge would have been aghast at the suggestion that his clerk receive such "charity.") However, the rationale of providing time off includes not only the human needs of the workforce but also the premise that productivity and efficiency will increase if the workforce is healthy, rested, and stable.

Kinds of Leave

Since employees will "require" time for different purposes, it is necessary to define the terms and purposes of each type of leave, establish amounts, and outline a system of accrual.

VACATION. Vacation can be described simply as time away from work; its purpose is to provide the worker with a period of rest and diversion for his own benefit and hopefully to the end of increasing efficiency and productivity on the job. In many cases the amount of vacation will vary with length of service and/or position. For instance, nonmanagement personnel might have two weeks of vacation per year and an increase to three weeks after five years of employment and to four weeks after ten years. Management or professional personnel might start with three weeks of vacation with similar increases. It is an accepted practice to assign more vacation time to jobs with higher levels of responsibility, since the management and professional employees who fit into that category often work long hours under pressure conditions with no additional financial compensation.

As to methods of accruing vacation time, there are several approaches, and most of them in some way reflect the principle of "earning time." In some cases vacation is earned in blocks—two weeks after one year of service or one week after six months employment. In others it is accumulated on a prorated basis; for instance, an employee eligible for 2 weeks, or 80 hours, of vacation per year would accrue 6.67 hours per month.

SICK LEAVE. Sick leave should be clearly defined to delineate its acceptable uses: employee's illness, illness in the immediate family, employee's appointments with doctors and/or dentists, and health-related appointments for members of the employee's family. The point is to consider the alternatives and define uses.

The means of accrual is another important consideration. Some accrual system is necessary to provide compensation for employees who are incapacitated by a serious illness or non-work-related injury. Sick leave can be accrued as it is earned, with a maximum accrual, for example, one day a month to a maximum of 30 days. Or employees can be given a "bank" of sick leave that is increased at scheduled intervals, such as 5 days at the end of 3 months and an additional 5 days each quarter thereafter to a maximum of 30 or 60 days. In either case employees who had accrued the maximum would be able to replenish any used sick leave by continuing the accrual process at the normal rate. If health insurance or disability coverage starts after a waiting period, the sick leave policy should complement the insurance plan.

HOLIDAYS. Employees expect to have days to celebrate community-recognized occasions. There are standard days that are almost universal—Christmas, Thanksgiving Day, New Year's Day, Labor, Memorial, and Independence Days, and Washington's Birthday. Others will vary according to location—Patriot's Day in Boston, Columbus Day, the birthdays of Robert E. Lee, Abraham Lincoln, and Martin Luther King, Gasparilla Day in Tampa. Because some organizations, such as health-care facilities, have special scheduling problems, they find it better to have a minimum number of fixed holidays and to give "floating holidays," employee birthdays, personal days, and the like s that staffing problems can be eased without short-changing the staff or services. Still others find it more advantageous to both management and staff to schedule holidays to provide more long weekends, such as the Friday after Thanksgiving.

BEREAVEMENT LEAVE. Although it is fitting to recognize the individual's need for time off when a close relative dies, there are variables and alternatives that should be considered prospectively. The employee's relation to the deceased person should determine whether he is eligible for leave and possibly the amount of leave due. It is customary to grant bereavement leave only for the death of a relative, but even the term "relative" should be defined—spouse, child, grandparent, parent, sibling, in-law, aunt, uncle, cousin. Some companies grant differing amounts of time depending on the degree of relation—perhaps three days for members of the immediate family and one day for other relatives. Another variable is the provision of extra time if the services are held at a distant location such as outside a radius of 500 miles.

JURY DUTY. In the spirit of community action, most organizations provide an employee with time to serve on jury, unless the employee is performing an indispensable service, and pay the difference between jury duty and the employee's normal wage.

LEAVES WITHOUT PAY. Leaves without pay can be requested for such specific purposes as education, maternity, and military service and also for a host of personal reasons ranging from extra vacation time to medical problems or family obligations. In any case, it is necessary to have well-defined policies establishing maximum amounts of leave, such as three or six months, and acceptable reasons for the time off. In the case of military and maternity leaves, it is necessary to comply with state and federal legislation and guidelines (see Chapter 9).

PERSONAL LEAVE. With the conviction that employees are going to take the time anyway, some employers grant a limited amount of time off for personal use. It may be three days per year that can be taken in specified blocks of time such as a minimum of three hours at a time. If personal time off is granted, it is important to have guidelines that will prevent workers from using it to cover themselves for tardiness, long lunches, early departures, and the like. Beyond that, within the administrative limitations set for use of leave, the time may be taken for any purpose from tending to family obligations to shopping.

Administrative Rules

The key to any set of time-off policies is a workable plan for administering the benefits. It is necessary first to define eligibility and then to determine the guidelines for using leave.

ELIGIBILITY. There are two issues to consider to determine eligibility: which categories of employees will be eligible for time off and when they will be eligible to use the benefit. There are four categories of employees.

1. Full-time permanent. This includes employees who are hired to work a full schedule, such as 40 hours a week. They will be eligible for all time-off benefits.

2. Part-time permanent. Those who are hired to work less than a full schedule, such as 20 or 30 hours a week, fit into this category. The usual way to accommodate the group is to prorate time off in proportion to the schedule. If, for instance, the regular workweek is 40 hours, the person who works 20 hours will receive 50 percent of the full-timer's benefit. Most employers require that an individual work a minimum number of hours, usually 16 to 20, to qualify for time off.

3. Temporary. Full- or part-time employees are temporary when they are hired to work for a specific period of time, usually less than the probationary period. People hired for a peak period, like the Christmas rush, income tax season, vacation relief, or special projects fall into this classification. These employees are usually ineligible for any time off with the possible exception of holidays.

4. Casual. People who work on an occasional and irregular basis are casual employees. Usually such individuals are paid only for time worked and receive no benefits.

The waiting period an employee must observe before being eligible to use leave must also be determined. Permanent employees generally are eligible to receive sick pay only after the probationary period has been completed. There is usually a longer waiting period before employees can use vacation time— six months, a year, or after a certain number of hours have been worked. In the case of leave without pay, freedom to establish waiting periods is restricted when such leave is for military or maternity purposes. Individuals with military commitments, such as summer camp or National Guard obligations, must be given time to fulfill their responsibilities. Maternity leave has been the subject of much controversy and many court decisions and is subject to change (see Chapter 9); it is wise to review maternity leave policy with the Equal Employment Opportunity Commission before publicizing it to employees.

USING LEAVE. Just as time off is important to employees, the control of its use is vital to the continuing function of any organization. Good order demands development and publication of appropriate rules governing the use of leave. Eleven topics should be considered.

1. Requests for leave. Requests for leave should be made in

advance so that management can take appropriate steps to organize the work and maintain adequate staffing. There should be a time frame for requesting leave; ordinarily leave should be requested at least two weeks in advance. It may be advisable to require that such requests, especially for leaves without pay, be written. Most employers consider employees who do not request leave in advance to be absent without leave (AWOL); individuals who are AWOL usually receive no compensation for the time and might be subject to further discipline.

2. Conflicting requests. To avoid the staffing and personal problems that can occur when two or more employees from the same area request simultaneous leaves, it is helpful to devise a system which will foster advance planning and provide a measure of control over last-minute requests. A notice may be circulated periodically or before popular vacation times, that is, June through September, asking employees to make vacation requests by a reasonable deadline. That will give supervisors time to identify possible conflicts and work out solutions with a minimum of inconvenience to the employees.

If conflicts do occur, the ideal solution is to explain the situation to those concerned to see if they themselves can resolve the issue. If not, an objective ruling must be made to honor one request over another, perhaps according to date of request or employee seniority. Employees who do not respond by the deadline date will be given last preference. Of course, the same criteria must be used in solving all conflicts.

3. Vacation cutoff. Workers should be encouraged to use vacation rather than hoard unused time. In that light and to prevent the staffing and financial complications that occur when employees who have accumulated substantial amounts of leave either want to use the time in large blocks or must be paid for unused leave when terminating, many companies set an accrual limit. In most cases, they do so by establishing a date by which leave must be used, perhaps December 31 of the following year. Any leave not taken by that time is lost unless the employee was specifically requested not to take vacation time for the company's convenience.

4. Call-in procedures. Employees who find it necessary to take sick or bereavement leave should call their supervisors by the

start of the shift at the latest. Employees on sick leave may be required to call in every day unless a predictably long absence or hospitalization is involved. Again, employees who fail to observe publicized procedures may be considered AWOL.

5. Commencement of sick leave. Some employers choose to begin pay with the first day of absence. Others, in an effort to discourage employees from abusing sick leave, commence sick pay from the second day of absence. Still others compromise by starting sick pay on the second day for newer employees and on the first day for employees with longer service, such as one to five years.

6. Medical documentation. Medical statements can be required either as proof of illness or evidence that an employee is physically able to work. Requiring medical certification can be effective in correcting sick leave abuse and can help to eliminate liability, particularly when there is a potential workmen's compensation claim.

7. Unused leave. The most common issue regarding unused leave involves the terminating employee. It is customary to include on the final check payment for unused vacation time. Many employers have a policy that such payment will be made only to the employee who leaves in good standing, that is, one who has resigned with notice; thus disciplinary terminations and those who quit without notice are excluded. In some instances, particularly when collective bargaining contracts are involved, employees are paid for unused sick time, either when terminating or as an annual "bonus." Those are rare instances, and they negate the underlying reason for providing sick time: to insure continued earnings during illness.

8. Returning from leave without pay. The use of an extended leave without pay presents special problems. In most cases, an employee going on an extended leave must be replaced. The employer has a double problem: he must make sure that the function continues, and he has no guarantee that the individual will return. Since it is usually impossible to recruit a competent employee on a temporary or indefinite basis, the general practice is to assure the employee that, if he wishes to return to work at the end of his leave, every effort will be made to place him in the same position or a comparable one (see Chapter 9). When an

employee is ready to return to work, he should notify his supervisor by a certain date, say, two or three weeks before his intended date of return.

9. Effects of leave without pay. Leaves without pay affect such employee benefits as seniority, vacation and sick leave accrual, and eligibility for raises and insurance. A balanced approach is to consider the leave period as a suspension rather than a break of service. An employee would not accrue any time off or seniority while on leave but would resume the accrual process and eligibility for benefits as soon as he returned to work; he would continue his eligibility for most insurance benefits at his own expense; and wage review dates would be adjusted to reflect the time spent on leave. Since the effect of maternity leave on seniority has been the subject of several court cases, the effect of such policies on employees who take extended maternity leave should be discussed with an attorney on the Equal Employment Opportunity Commission.

10. Restrictions. Sometimes it is necessary to restrict the use of leave. For instance, if the nature of the work requires full staffing at peak times, as during income tax periods for accounting firms or the Christmas rush for retailers, it may be necessary to restrict vacations at those times. Some employers also require that employees report for work as scheduled on the days preceding and following holidays. Leaves without pay, except for military and maternity leaves, may be restricted to employees with satisfactory work records. The important thing is to publicize such restrictions well in advance and administer the policies without discrimination or favoritism.

11. Incentive plans. To discourage unnecessary use of sick leave, many employers devise incentive systems that reward employees for not abusing the benefit. In one such system the employee is given a time bonus, say, one day of personal leave per quarter without latenesses or sick time. Other systems provide for a prize or bonus in a kind of lottery for which all employees who meet attendance standards are eligible. Standards vary—no sick leave or absences for the quarter, no use of any leave for a month—as do the prizes, which can be a gift certificate, savings bond, fixed-dollar bonus, or gift object of some kind.

INSURED BENEFITS

Insured benefits * represent a sizable expenditure for the employer and have a substantial financial impact on employees. Since the wrong benefit program can backfire for the employer in terms of employee relations value and can be catastrophic to the individual, all plans should be weighed for the extent of coverage, the insurer's acceptability in the community, and claims service as well as for cost. Moreover, it is vital to assure the long-term viability of insurance programs. Since insured benefits are highly visible to the workforce, changes in insurers are likely to cause concern, lack of security, accusations of instability, and even fear among workers. Care also must be taken to avoid disruption of coverage with accompanying loss of benefits.

Decisions regarding insured benefits must be made with an eye toward need, resources, and legal implications to the organization. Self-insured programs should not be approached lightly. Although they are viewed by some as a means of providing a benefit without a structured payment program, in effect they risk the organization's capital in a very real way and ought to be financed by setting aside reserves that reflect actuarial risk calculations. Since an individual group is a much smaller sample than the number of people covered by an insurance company, self-insuring can be substantially more expensive. Operating with inadequate reserves can be disastrous if a number of claims come due in a short period of time.

Kinds of Insured Benefits

Employee benefit packages typically are combinations of life and health insurance, disability coverage, and retirement income programs. The extent of the benefit, the size and sex-age composition of the group, and in some instances geographic location determine cost.

LIFE INSURANCE. Life insurance can be purchased on a group basis either in flat amounts or as a percent of salary. The employer can cover the whole cost (noncontributory) or can share the cost with the employee (contributory). It is unlikely

---

* For purposes of this discussion the term "insured benefits" refers to any plan that involves special funding and reserves that assume availability of claim payment. Thus trust funds and self-insured programs are considered "insured." A distinction is made to describe *insurance* benefits.

that an insurance company would write a contract under which employees would pay the entire cost.

The cheapest rate probably will be quoted for a noncontributory policy with a flat amount of coverage for each employee and eligibility requirements that guarantee a high level of participation. Rates will be inversely proportional to the size of the group. If coverage is optional rather than automatic, rates will increase. The theory is that the risk is higher, since those who elect coverage will be more likely to become claimants.

It is common for companies to have one policy that covers all employees or nonmanagement personnel and a second, more liberal, policy for executives or management personnel. That is a legitimate and acceptable practice provided it does not discriminate against minority employees.

HEALTH INSURANCE. There are a great many variables within health insurance, and premiums naturally increase with coverage. The most restrictive, and cheapest, coverage is the indemnity policy that specifies the amount allowed for each item covered, such as doctors' hospital visits $10, appendectomy $250. Because the coverage and demand are so limited, insurance companies are not anxious to write such policies in most geographic areas. The more typical health insurance plan covers hospital costs for semiprivate accommodations, inpatient X-ray and laboratory studies, emergency room treatment within 72 hours, and "usual and customary" doctors' fees for hospital visits, radiation therapy, and similar expenses.

Optional coverage can be extended to include outpatient procedures, including treatments and office visits for illness and prescriptions for therapeutic drugs. Items such as those often are subject to a "deductible" such as $75, which the insured pays before costs are picked up by the insurance company; most times 80 percent of charges above the deductible are paid by the insurer, and the insured is responsible for the other 20 percent. Coverage is almost always limited to treatment for an illness or condition rather than to preventive measures such as annual physicals, birth control, and vaccinations.

Other variances include coverage for psychiatric illness, maternity benefits,* dental insurance, maximum benefit

* EEOC guidelines require that all female employees receive maternity coverage regardless of marital status.

amount, benefit periods, and amounts of deductible. In order to lower premiums, some insurers are getting away from the traditional concept of covering all inpatient charges and having a "major medical" system for other costs. Instead, they have designed a policy under which all charges are subject to a higher deductible, say $200 per person, with a maximum liability to the insured.

The best way to compare coverage is simply to make a grid listing each type of service, the extent of coverage, the employee liability, and cost. As with every expenditure, the point is to get the best value for money spent. In the case of insurance, many employees would prefer to expand coverage and contribute more toward the cost themselves.

In contrast to the insurance policy, the health maintenance organization (HMO) is designed not to pay for treatment of illness but to provide ongoing health services, including preventive medicine, to their members. The theory, of course, is that it is cheaper to prevent than to treat illness.

Federal legislation (see Chapter 9) specifies the parameters which qualify an HMO; the aim is the assurance of broad coverage to members. Hence, the HMO must provide both inpatient and outpatient care, prescription services, proscribed physician services, preventive dental care for children, ancillary services including diagnostic laboratory and X-ray and therapeutic X-ray facilities, and medical treatment and referral services for drug and alcohol addiction.

The aim of the HMO system is to provide comprehensive services with a maximum of efficiency and a minimum of cost. Employers are not required to pay more for HMO membership than they would ordinarily pay for employee health insurance. Enrollees may be charged for additional nominal copayments to supplement basic health service payments, normally when services are received. Reimbursements are made to HMO members who secure medically necessary treatment on a fee-for-service basis if they are unable to secure HMO services first.

DISABILITY INSURANCE. Insurance is available for short- or long-term disabilities. Disability insurance is designed to provide income to the disabled employee after sick leave has been exhausted. Short-term disability begins after a brief waiting period, usually two to four weeks, and is paid for a limited amount of time, usually up to six months. It covers non-employment-related illnesses or injuries such as a broken leg, recuperation from serious surgery, or a heart attack. Long-term disability covers the more catastrophic disability; benefits usually commence after a waiting period of six months or more. To dovetail with income tax exemptions, such insurance typically provides a percent of the employee's income, often with a maximum monthly benefit and maximum benefit period. Again, premiums vary with the amount of coverage. Insurers tend to write short-term policies only on a noncontributory basis.

ACCIDENTAL DEATH AND DISMEMBERMENT. Coverage for accidental death or dismemberment provides lump sum payments if an individual is accidentally killed or suffers loss of a member—eye, arm, finger—through an accident. Typically, the face amount of the policy is collectible if death is involved and specified lesser amounts are payable for dismemberments. Premiums generally are flat amounts per thousand dollars of coverage and, because the actuarial risks are lower, less than those for other forms of life insurance.

RETIREMENT INCOME PLANS. Obviously, the aim of a retirement income program is to provide the retired person with a continuing income that will support continued living on a standard comparable with preretirement style. Under the present tax structure and with the constantly rising cost of living, it is unlikely that even high-income individuals would be able to save enough money at high enough interest rates to be able to provide such an income for themselves. In addition, retirement programs provide a sizable tax benefit to employees, since the income from a qualified plan is taxable only when received and not during the period of employment when, presumably, the earnings would have been subject to a higher tax rate. Since death benefits and survivor payments under such programs often are taxed on a different basis than other kinds of inheritances, there is also a meaningful benefit to heirs.

From the employer's point of view, however, retirement income programs have complex legal and financial ramifications and involve complex and technical considerations. Beyond the obvious cost factor, a prime example is the plan's conformance to the standards set forth by the Employee's Retirement Income Security Act of 1974 (ERISA), which regulates all phases of such plans from eligibility to funding requirements. All plans must qualify under ERISA standards. Once an employer has determined that he can establish a retirement program, there is the question of selecting the right kind of plan and determining the appropriate benefit levels.

In general, there are three approaches to retirement programs: pensions, profit sharing, and stock bonus programs.

1. Pensions. Pension programs entail a systematic payment of monies to provide determinable benefits at retirement age. Typically they involve an insurance contract or the establishment of a trust fund, each of which can be designed with a number of variations. Insurance plans, for instance, can involve the annual purchase of annuities for individual employees (Group Annuity Plan), the deposit of appropriate sums into a general fund from which monies are withdrawn to purchase annuities when an employee retires (Deposit Administration Plan), or the purchase of substantial amounts of endowment-type life insurance that will be paid to the employee in installments commencing with retirement (Group Permanent Pension Plan).

Pension trusts are funds set aside under a formal trust agreement, along with the income derived from those monies, in amounts sufficient, by actuarial standards, to pay prescribed benefit levels. They can be established as general funds from which the trustee pays benefits as employees retire or as individual-policy pension trusts used to purchase substantial amounts of life insurance to be converted to annuities at retirement.

The choice of such a plan or combination of plans will vary with the circumstances of the organization, including size. The smaller company, for instance, may find it best to opt for the individual-policy pension trust or group permanent pension plan, since neither approach requires a minimal number of participants.

In any case it may be advisable to investigate the availability of retirement programs through a larger, special-interest group which may provide wider benefit options at a considerable savings. Some educators, for instance, may be eligible for inclusion in a teachers' annuity program.

2. Profit sharing. In a profit-sharing retirement program, the employer establishes a trust fund into which he contributes, ac-

cording to a prescribed formula, a share of profits for accumulation and investment to be distributed to employees at retirement. No payments are made into the fund unless the specified profit levels are met.

3. Stock bonuses. Stock bonus programs are similar to profit-sharing plans in that all contributions are made by the employer, usually from profits. The difference is that, instead of contributing cash, the employer sets aside shares of stock for each eligible employee in conformance with an established formula. Retirement income takes the form of dividends or the sale of stock.

Administration

Whether a program of insured benefits is successful in terms of its impact on employees and employee-management relations and whether costs are controllable for the employer often depend on how well the program is administered. There are four areas on which to focus.

RULES. Most of the rules governing participation in insured benefits are incorporated into contracts or plans drawn up by carriers or trustees. Some are the subject of law, as in the case of ERISA's regulation of the eligibility and vesting requirements of pension plans. In any event, the employer should be aware of the topics for which rules and procedures should be established.

1. Eligibility. One of the first questions to be decided is who will be eligible for benefits. Employees should be grouped into the same categories that are used to establish time-off policies—full-time permanent, part-time permanent, full-time temporary, part-time temporary, and casual. Ordinarily only permanent employees, and for the most part full-timers, are eligible for insured benefits. The common exception is for health insurance, which some employers extend to part-time personnel who work a specified minimum number of hours and pay an additional share of the cost.

2. Waiting periods. Employees usually are required to have been employed for specified lengths of time before being eligible for benefits. Health insurance usually has the shortest waiting period, ordinarily 30 days. Other times vary from 60 to 90 days for life insurance, six months for disability programs, to one year for retirement plans (for employees 25 years or older). For some benefits, part-time employees may be required to work a

specified number of hours before becoming eligible. A part-timer, for instance, might be required to work 173 hours, or the equivalent of 30 days of full-time employment, before becoming eligible for health insurance.

3. Changes in status. Special rules should be established to cover situations in which eligibility for benefits changes because the employee changes his employment status. For instance, a change from temporary to permanent or from part-time to full-time status may affect eligibility for insurance, or may cause benefit levels to increase concomitantly with salary increases. It's usually easiest to make the change in coverage effective on the first of the month following the change in status.

4. Reinstatement. Former participants who are rehired within a short time, say, 90 days, or those whose employment status temporarily excluded them from coverage should not have to observe the normal waiting period before being reinstated in insurance programs. Usually they are covered as of the first of the month following their reemployment.

5. Leaves. Employees who are on leave without pay often are permitted to continue their life and health insurance coverage at their own expense during the leave period, as are those temporarily laid off.

6. Cost sharing. Determining the employees' share of insurance coverage has budgetary plus employee relations implications. It is particularly common to share health insurance premiums. Normally, the employer pays at least one-half the cost of individual coverage. In some cases the employee is expected to cover the cost of dependent coverage; in others the employer pays some part of the difference. When premiums are increased, most organizations try to absorb the additional cost.

CONTRACT ADMINISTRATION. Broadly speaking, insurance can be administered by either the employer or the insurance company (or trustee). Under self-administered contracts the employer is responsible for all record keeping, billing, claims submissions, and so on. The carrier merely adjusts and pays claims, usually through the employer. The alternative is a system in which all forms, enrollment, termination, and change-of-status information is sent to the insurer or trustee, as are requests for beneficiary or name changes and the like. Claims forms also are sent directly to the carrier by employees, and payments are made to employees with no company involvement. Each month the employer receives a bill reflecting the enrollment-termination activity he has reported.

Since a self-administered plan involves a lower cost for the carrier, premiums often are lower for such a contract. However, depending on the size of the organization, the saving can be more than offset by the expense of handling the matter on an in-house basis. If an additional person must be hired to perform the clerical work or if the program's supervision must be added to the responsibilities of a busy manager, it may be cheaper in the long run to have the carrier administer the plan. On the other hand, controlling the billing procedure within the organization and increasing services and responsiveness to the workforce may compensate for the extra work and expense of a self-administered plan.

COST CONTAINMENT. There are two keys to cost containment in the administration of insured benefits. One is to establish efficient systems to coordinate payroll deductions and terminations from the plan and the other is to limit claims experience.

It is essential to develop an accurate system for commencing employee payroll deductions as soon as coverage begins. If insurance deduction information can be fed into a computerized payroll system with the initial "hire data," the problem is substantially reduced. However, there are few such facilities outside large corporations with sophisticated payroll and personnel data systems, and there are many variables in securing timely employee enrollment.

The first step is to emphasize prompt enrollment of all interested employees and expeditious delivery of the enrollment forms to the employee responsible for processing such material. It is advisable to have all clerical work, such as premium calculations and payroll forms, completed at once. A dated *suspense,* or *follow-up,* file system can be set up either in that department or in the payroll section so that the information can be processed when the payroll for the appropriate pay period is processed. Depending on the insurance package and the payroll system, that may require a number of payroll deduction notices to be processed at different dates; for example, health insurance might be processed on January 1, life insurance on March 1, and disability insurance on June 1. But if the clerical work is done in advance and filed as described above, there is less margin for error. Similarly, benefits administration personnel must be notified to terminate noneligible employees from the plan as soon as possible. Limiting claims experience on which premium rates are based is no easy task, although many approaches have been used. Some companies require employment physicals to screen out illness problems that would prevent an individual from performing his job or to discover health problems that can be controlled. Others require periodic physicals or have employee health service personnel conduct health and hygiene education programs for the workforce. Some even award bonuses to their workers if claims experience is low enough to contain premium rates.

For the typical employer whose resources are limited, experience-control efforts may be restricted to distribution of flyers or brochures supplied by insurance companies, community health agencies, or safety institutes and general encouragement of good health and safety practices. The employer whose group has received several premium increases because of high experience factors may find it worthwhile to analyze what kind of claims have been processed under the contract with an eye toward directing a campaign against the specific causes.

EMPLOYEE EDUCATION AND SERVICES. To maximize the employee relations value of benefits, it is essential to provide employees with adequate information concerning their coverage and options and a resource within the organization to answer specific questions and assist them with claims and other problems.

Although most insurers provide booklets and/or certificates explaining coverage, employee education must go beyond that. Not only are most people confused by insurance policies and the technical wording used in many brochures, but many do not understand the fine points in such related issues as the designation of minors as life insurance beneficiaries, establishing a deductible sum under major-medical-type coverage, and the concept of preexisting conditions. Therefore, special efforts should be made to explain the coverage to all employees, perhaps as part of an orientation program. Supervisors should be given supplementary training so that they can answer general questions. In addition, there should be some individual who is well versed in such matters and is available to answer questions and assist employees on a routine basis.

If a contract is self-administered, special care should be taken in processing claims. All claims forms should be reviewed to assure completeness and clarity. A logbook should be maintained to record claims information including employee's name, date of receipt, date forwarded to insurer, nature and amount of claim, date the claim was settled, amount of settlement, and miscellaneous information including requests for supplemental information. Periodic follow-up contacts with the insurer should be made if claims have not been settled within the normal processing time.

Occasionally, unanticipated problems interfere with employee utilization of coverage. For instance, hospitals unfamiliar with certain plans or insurers may refuse to accept assignments of benefits when employees or their dependents are treated or admitted. Often that difficulty can be resolved by a telephone call or letter to the person in charge of patient financial services or billing departments. If such facilities are furnished with a copy of a brochure or list of services covered, along with the name and telephone number of an individual who can verify coverage, they are likely to correct the problem.

One additional point should be emphasized. Employees should be enrolled promptly. If a new plan is put into effect, control lists should be established to make sure that all employees are offered coverage. If coverage is declined, especially under a noncontributory contract, the employee should sign a card refusing the benefit. If a plan is in effect, new employees should sign an enrollment or refusal card as soon as possible. Again, control lists or checklists should be used to make sure that no one is overlooked.

Such procedures are important for two reasons. First, most policies and plans require that employees who do not enroll within 30 days of becoming eligible must supply "evidence of insurability," including a very specific medical questionnaire and possibly a medical examination, or must wait for an open enrollment period. Second, it is advisable to keep evidence of refusal to disprove liability or refute possible charges that the organization discriminated by not offering benefits to certain individuals.

ADDITIONAL BENEFITS

For organizational purposes it is expeditious to categorize additional benefits to be discussed into those that are legally required and those that are optional, that is, that are neither required by law nor necessarily included in the basic benefit package offered in the typical employment situation.

Legally Required Benefits

Although employers and workers alike frequently limit their conceptions of benefits to the time-off and insured benefits described above, other benefits that belong in such a discussion include some often omitted simply because they are required by law. There are three such benefits:

1. Federal Social Security. Social Security provides for a shared tax on the income of each employee who receives more than $50 in wages per quarter. Effective January 1, 1979, the tax was set at 12.26 percent of the first $22,900 of income, and 6.13 percent of the individual's income is deducted from each pay check. A corresponding amount is paid by the employer. The taxable salary base will be increased to $25,900 as of January 1, 1980.

2. Unemployment compensation. This benefit is discussed in full in Chapter 9. It is listed here to highlight this employer expense as an employee benefit.

3. Workmen's compensation. See Chapter 9.

One other service performed by the employer—federal and state income tax withholding—is seldom, if ever, listed as a benefit. Although federal law requires that income tax be withheld and deposited quarterly on the employee's behalf, that is a service performed at some cost: expenses involved in record keeping, payroll processing, and other bookkeeping or accounting procedures. The fact that the service is performed for him saves the employee the time and trouble to which he would otherwise be subjected. In effect, it is a savings plan that allows the employee to pay his taxes with a minimum of difficulty.

Optional Benefits

The list of optional benefits that can be used to "ice the cake" is a long one. In formulating the optional segment of the benefits program it is essential to design a package that will be affordable, provide a return on the investment, and be well received by employees.

In considering costs, it is important not to overlook the sometimes hidden problems of administering the benefit—cost of clerical time, file space, supplies, phone bills—and the logistics of record keeping. For example, can the payroll system accommodate an additional deduction report to record an employees' savings program? Plans also should be examined for possible negative repercussions. A tuition program, for instance, may provide an education that will equip an employee for a career in areas outside the sphere of the organization's activities and thereby contribute to turnover. In addition, benefits must be usable by the workforce, and not be mere window dressing.

One final note is important. Benefits are part of the terms and conditions of employment, and they therefore come under the legislative umbrella. As a result, benefit programs must be examined to eliminate any unintentional discrimination. That is particularly true of benefits that have an impact on the financial well-being of employees.

BONUSES. There are a number of systems for providing bonuses to employees. Some companies give annual bonuses to all employees at Christmas or at the end of the fiscal year; others establish bonuses for executive or management personnel. Some bonuses are computed on complicated formulas that reflect departmental or corporate earnings or length of service; some are a percent of income either fixed throughout the organization or assigned to position; some are a flat amount; and some are designed as part of an incentive compensation system to reflect the employee's performance or impact on profits.

Any direct payment of monies is welcome to the workforce. It is important to note, however, that once a bonus is distributed to them, employees come to expect it on an annual basis. Therefore, no bonus should be given without anticipating that expectation.

PROFIT SHARING (CASH DISTRIBUTION). Profit sharing on a cash distribution basis is much like that described for retirement income plans except that monies are distributed in cash at the end of the fiscal year instead of being deposited in a fund. Such distributions are made only when profits reach prescribed levels and are calculated according to a specified formula. Since no fund or deferred payment plan is involved, a cash distribution program is not subject to ERISA regulations.

EMPLOYEE STOCK PURCHASE PLANS. Many companies have plans under which employees can purchase stock in the corporation directly through the company on advantageous terms. Although the mechanisms vary, the principle behind such plans is to reserve stock for purchase by employees at a fixed price, usually the closing market price on a specified trading day. Employees commit themselves to purchase the number of shares they designate within prescribed limits, or they may reserve a number of shares for possible purchase within a specified length of time. Payment may be made through payroll deduction.

Stock purchase plans must be approved by the Securities and Exchange Commission before they are offered to employees, and they are subject to close inspection and regulation.

SAVINGS PLANS. Arrangements can be made to make payroll deductions for purchase of U.S. savings bonds or for deposit into bank savings accounts. That kind of program involves no cash outlay, but it can create administrative problems of record keeping, deposits, and employee service. (Consider the employee who will want to skip such deductions on a chronic or even an occasional basis.)

CREDIT UNIONS. A popular program is the formation of credit unions within companies. Employees generally join credit unions by purchasing a number of shares through payroll deduction. The monies are deposited in an interest-earning account and form a pool from which members can borrow at a low rate of interest. Employees gain two benefits: a systematic method of saving and the opportunity to borrow at low interest rates without disturbing their capital. Reserves must be established and guidelines set up to regulate the amounts of and purposes for loans; all such transactions must be approved by the credit union's board of directors.

Credit unions are subject to federal legislation and involve a number of cost items for the employer including office and file space, payroll expenses for credit union personnel, payment for time not worked by employees on the board while they are transacting credit union business, the services of the manager or executive responsible for the credit union, and miscellaneous expenses like supplies and telephone bills.

EDUCATION ASSISTANCE. There are a number of ways to set up educational assistance plans: direct payment, reimbursement, loans to employees, or even scholarship programs. Probably the most popular is the tuition refund plan. Whichever approach is selected, a series of administrative rules must be drawn up to regulate the program:

1. Eligibility, including status of employee, length of service, and performance standards.
2. Application mechanisms and approving signatures.
3. Time limitations, that is, a limit on the number of courses to be taken per semester.
4. Satisfactory completion of the course.
5. Extent of coverage, for example, tuition only, tuition and textbooks, dollar limits.
6. Course relevancy, that is, whether any course will be covered or the course material must be relevant to the individual's work in some way.

There are a number of ramifications to be considered from the employer's perspective before an educational assistance program is established; basically they relate to whether such a program will benefit or disadvantage the employer. Certainly it does not make sense to put out substantial sums to train employees in fields not relevant or useful to the employing organization. Beyond that there is the question of raising the employee's expectations in terms of his own perception of the value of his training to the organization or the availability of advancement at the completion of training. If salary programs and promotional channels do not provide for such advancement, the employee is likely to seek greener pastures.

As a result, many employers prefer to provide for employee education by sending individuals to professional seminars or selected courses that would not only add to the individuals' skills and credentials but also have an immediate positive effect on performance in current or prospective positions. Still another approach is to provide scholarship funds for the children of employees, possibly on a competitive basis of some kind.

MATCHING GIFTS. Some employers have a system of making a charitable contribution in an employee's name that is equal to the contribution made by the employee himself. Frequently such a gift is limited to an educational institution, and it gives the employer a possible added benefit by providing early exposure to prospective recruits. For employers with projected recruiting needs, that can be a real plus.

PAYMENT FOR TIME NOT WORKED. Although frequently overlooked, payment for time not worked can amount to a considerable expenditure and should be classified as an employee benefit. Into this category fall breaks, time spent on union business or pursuing such employee social activities as newspaper contributions, picnics, social committees, and special-occasion lunches, paid time spent in personal preparation for or cleanup from work, pursuing grievances, and traveling between work sites.

DISCOUNTS. Employers often arrange for employees to purchase their own goods at a reduced price. Similar or reciprocal arrangements can be made with interested organizations in the community. For instance, some toy and craft stores offer a discount to teachers in an effort to encourage the purchase of materials used in the classrooms. In addition, there are companies that specialize in providing discount-purchasing systems on a commission basis. If an employee wants to purchase a specific product, often a major item like a car or appliance, he can give the discount company information concerning the make and model he desires. The discount firm will then supply him with the name of a dealer who will offer the item at a discount and pay the firm for the referral. The employer assumes no liability and no costs; he merely posts the name of the discount firm or makes brochures available to the workers.

TRAVEL PLANS. Travel agencies often look to employers as a market for group tours, which furnish travel opportunities at reduced rates. Ordinarily they are happy to have the employer publicize a tour or trip if there is a likelihood that a minimal number of employees will sign up. Since all arrangements are made through the travel agency, there is little employer involvement except for publicity and possibly some liaison work. However, the benefit should not be offered if operations will be adversely affected by having a group of employees on leave at the same time or if employees tend not to have the financial cushion needed for such luxuries.

AWARDS. There are a number of awards that can be made to

employees; they include monetary awards for suggestions, awards or gifts for significant employment anniversaries (5, 10, 15, 20, 25 years of service), and prizes for production contests and similar events.

CHILD CARE. With the increased number of women in the workforce and the inclusion of domestic employees under the ever-rising minimum wage, the provision of day-care facilities is a benefit worth consideration. That is particularly true in industries, like health care, that rely heavily on female employees. Day care requires provision of facilities, meals, and supervision, and approval by the local board of health is necessary.

TRANSPORTATION. Providing transportation for employees can be a key benefit. Many large employers developed bus services in conjunction with affirmative-action or energy conservation programs, but even some small organizations not easily accessible to public transportation have furnished shuttle service between the work site and the nearest transportation stop. Others have provided informal lifts to workers on second or third shifts or in extreme weather.

PARKING. Depending on location, the availability of public transportation, the need for independent mobility, and the nature of the workforce, provision of free or subsidized employee parking is an important consideration.

PUBLICITY

Beyond providing employees with basic information regarding benefits and the use of benefits, it is appropriate and often necessary for employers to publicize benefits and the costs incurred in supplying them. In some cases, it is essential to sell a benefit. In assessing publicity needs, two topics must be addressed: the subject matter and the media to be used.

Subject Matter

Identifying topics that need special attention is a key to the success of any benefit program or publicity campaign. Any time a new benefit is added, some publicity is in order; whenever a personnel policy relating to benefits is changed, an effective means of informing the workforce must be developed; periodic reminders to employers that the organization supplies and pays for their benefits are in order because many workers take benefits for granted or do not realize that every benefit is a cost item for their employer. Publicity programs addressing those needs should promote understanding, acceptance, and appreciation.

Once again, there should be early involvement of the supervisory staff, who should receive special education in subject matter and publicity plans. Supervisors will not only reinforce information or enforce policy but also reflect employee reaction to both the substance and presentation.

Insured benefits require special attention. Even sophisticated and highly educated individuals frequently are confused by insurance contracts or policies or fail to take the time to study them. The problem is compounded among lower-level employees. Therefore, special efforts must be made to simplify explanations of such benefits and provide concrete examples of coverage and claims procedures.

Whenever employee money is involved, special efforts must be made to make the material understandable and acceptable. If employees are contributing to the cost of an insurance policy, they must know what their dollars are purchasing and how much the employer is contributing on an individual basis. If a benefit is designed to provide special financial incentive, as a profit-sharing plan does, the implications to the individual employee must be made clear.

Changes in timekeeping methods, systems for accruing leave, rules governing call-in procedures, eligibility for any benefit, even the relocation of parking places, must be explained. The first emphasis must be to make the new policy clear. Then the *reason* for the change must be explained. Employees tend to resist change, particularly when they feel that the change is due to a whim of management rather than a bona fide need. Next they must be convinced that they are not losing anything and, in fact, may stand to gain from the change.

A change in timekeeping methods, for instance, may be approached as follows:

1. Describe the new procedure.
2. Explain in simple terms the federal law which requires employers to observe certain standards *as a protection to employees.*
3. Show how the new system follows the law, eliminates inac-

curacies, speeds up payroll processing, works with computer, and so on.

4. Give examples of how pay checks (and overtime) will be calculated under the new system.

5. Reinforce the advantages to the worker of having accurate time-worked methods—correct pay checks, faster payment for overtime, or the like.

The important thing is to be correct and reasonable, anticipate the worker's fears and insecurities, and explain the advantage to both employer and employee.

Employees look at their pay checks in terms of take-home pay and forget the effects of benefits on their life style and security. An occasional reminder of what benefits do for the employee and how much they cost the employer is often helpful to employee-employer relations. A publicity campaign might demonstrate employer contributions to the legally required benefits, time not worked (including sick leave, vacations, and holidays), and insured and optional benefits.

Again, such information must be made meaningful to the employee. Emphasis can be placed either on the impact of the benefit on the employee or on the cost factors, but the approach must be concrete and specific. Health insurance can be highlighted by providing a list of typical expenses involved in an accident or maternity claim along with a breakdown of expenses the insurance would cover; pension plans can be dramatized by calculating anticipated monthly income if contributions were continued on the same basis until normal retirement age. A list of employer costs for each benefit can be computed for the average or individual employee, along with a figure showing the total companywide expenditures for benefits or the total expenditures for a specified segment of the workforce. If resources are available to provide each employee with information pertinent to him as an individual, so much the better; if average or "typical" figures are used, care should be taken to use figures within the range paid to the average employee.

Media

The means of publicizing benefits programs are as limited in number and diversity as the number and imagination of the people designing them. Within the framework of any medium, there is room for much innovation to produce the desired result while reflecting the image and personality of the organization.

BROCHURES AND BOOKLETS. To describe overall benefits programs to employees or provide comprehensive information about insured benefit plans, booklets and brochures are an effective tool. Many insurance companies provide, or will assist clients in designing, booklets describing coverage in an in-depth way. In fact, ERISA requires that the booklet be distributed to employees eligible for retirement income plans.

MEETINGS. Orientation programs for new personnel and special meetings to explain new benefits or changes in benefits or policies are invaluable since they offer an opportunity for questions and personalized explanation. If the material to be covered is technical or likely to evoke negative response, it is advisable to keep the groups as small as possible so that a more one-on-one approach can be used.

ILLUSTRATIONS. The use of graphic material is often effective. Charts, graphs, signs, photographs, posters, or even cartoons can illustrate data, depict specific situations, serve as reminders, evoke interest, build suspense, or create any of a multitude of effects.

HOUSE ORGANS. In-house publications can be used in many ways. Specific information regarding costs, benefit news, claims, procedures, experience data, and similar material can be included in such vehicles. Special features can be run on a regular basis to highlight a specific benefit. Or information can be provided to help reduce claims.

PAY CHECK INSERTS. General information or specific data about individual coverage and costs can be inserted into pay envelopes. The communication can be as informal as a mimeographed sheet or as official as a computerized report. *Everyone* opens the pay envelope.

SPECIAL EFFECTS. Special campaigns can include anything— perhaps "bankbooks" showing deferred payments or annual distribution of check facsimiles showing employer contributions for the year. One employer even arranged to pay employees in cash one payday. Each person received gross wages plus employer contributions at one window and went to a series of other windows to pay in cash the amount due for each benefit and/or tax paid on his behalf or deducted from his wages.

5 EMPLOYEE RELATIONS

Employee relations is the ongoing process of management interfacing with the workforce. Its goal is the creation of a well-ordered work environment by the establishment of a framework for management-employee relations. Thus, in addition to such matters as compensation and supervision, which are discussed elsewhere in this book, the employee relations function provides systems for processing employee-related transactions, establishes standards of behavior and equitable procedures for dealing with deviations from those systems, and routinizes record keeping.

EMPLOYEE INDUCTION PROCEDURES

Because an employee's first days on the job are critical to his perception of his job and employer and to his success in his position, it is important to make the whole process of induction and departmental orientation as smooth and efficient as possible.

As far as induction is concerned, the paperwork necessary for putting a new person on the payroll should be organized to expedite the process for the new employee as well as for the person responsible for processing the papers. Besides the obvious timesaving advantages, proper organization will help to insure that the new employee will, in fact, receive his first pay check. In addition, it will give him a sense of order.

The induction process can be efficient only if the preliminary papers and information are in order. All paperwork—applications, résumés, tests, references—should be kept together for each applicant under consideration; applications by those who are disqualified or unqualified should be filed immediately. There should be a system—handwritten note, mimeographed or printed form, specific places on the application—for informing the processor of starting date and salary, department, job title, replacement information, EEOC report data, and any other required information for successful candidates. All authorizing signatures should be secured before the starting date so that there can be no last-minute confusion or delay.

Tax forms, benefit enrollment cards and brochures, internal payroll forms, union enrollment cards, and other necessary documents should be at hand so new employees can complete them immediately. In a busy office all such material should be grouped in packets for ready use. To complete the process, the folder used for the personnel file should be prepared at the same time so the file is established and ready for filing and reference. When possible, the paperwork should be completed as soon as the employment offer is made and accepted.

Once on the job, each new employee must know how his job relates to other jobs and where and to whom he can go for assistance and information. Therefore, it is highly important to provide him with a well-ordered introduction to the personnel, structure, and physical layout of the department. Each department head or supervisor should work out a system to acquaint new personnel with the department. Orientation time should be set aside during the new employee's first hours on the job and, if necessary, on subsequent days. The work of the department as a whole should be explained, as should the department's place within the organization. The jobs of other personnel, particularly key members of the department, should be explained and individuals should be identified; perhaps outstanding physical characteristics, such as a mustache or long or short hair, may help the employee to remember key people. If the department or office is large, it may be useful to give the newcomer an organization chart or rough diagram of the physical layout along with names and titles.

Next, a tour of the department and introductions to coworkers are in order; during the tour much of the information presented initially should be reiterated so the employee can put faces, places, and facts together. Another employee may be asked to go to lunch with the newcomer and show him the location of coat closets, rest rooms, supplies, and so on. Of course, the new person's work station should have been cleaned, supplied, organized, and otherwise made ready for him; if possible, any backlog of work should be cleared up or assigned to other employees before he starts, so that he can learn his new job step by step without distraction or additional pressure.

If a job requires departmental interaction, the new worker should be told the names and job titles of the people with whom he will deal in other departments and then be introduced to those people. Because it is always difficult to remember people when they are introduced en masse, it is best to make the process gradual and meaningful; introductions and explanations might be made in one department a day or as the person is trained in that facet of his job. A general orientation to the organization should also be given in accordance with the criteria discussed in Chapter 8.

RULES AND REGULATIONS

Employees can meet expectations only if management formulates and communicates to them the standards and rules it deems necessary for the orderly functioning of the organization. Behavioral guidelines should be specified, and the penalties for infractions—grounds for immediate and possible discharge—should be delineated. Rules should be relevant to the operations and nature of the organization; they should be reasonable, objective, and enforceable. In addition, care must be taken to communicate them to the workforce in a suitable manner.

Relevance

Although circumstances may vary, there are certain broad categories of standards and rules which are common to almost all situations: the employee's conduct with the public, his relations with co-workers, safety and security, and job performance. Rules should be devised to cover those types of behavior.

CONDUCT WITH THE PUBLIC. Since employee behavior toward outsiders often will have a direct bearing on community acceptance, effective operations, and profits, rules governing public conduct are appropriate and necessary. They include the following areas:

1. Respect for clients—physical or verbal abuse, borrowing, soliciting tips, protection of privacy.
2. Disclosure of confidential information.
3. Giving advice, endorsements, and so on.
4. Dress or uniform regulations.

RELATIONS WITH CO-WORKERS. The interrelations of co-workers and the behavior of co-workers with one another determine the morale and efficiency of personnel. Since good order and teamwork depend on people working together, the following prohibitions might be included to foster harmony:

1. Fighting, horseplay, abusive language, gambling, and the like.
2. Collusion concerning records and timekeeping.
3. Soliciting contributions and so on.

SAFETY AND SECURITY. Rules designed to protect person and property involve employee, client, and management. In addition, good safety rules will help to insure conformance with OSHA requirements and minimize expenditures for workmen's compensation. The following are basic topics often included in such regulations:

1. Observance of fire regulations.
2. Smoking only in authorized areas—client consideration, hazardous areas or equipment, protection of records.
3. Observance of safety rules, including safe use of equipment and wiring and protective clothing and devices.
4. Possession of weapons.
5. Reporting to work under the influence of alcohol or drugs or possession of those substances on company property.

PERFORMANCE CRITERIA. It is wise to emphasize the requirement for conformance with performance and behavior criteria by including such topics as specific rules:

1. Satisfactory performance ratings.
2. Punctuality and attendance.
3. Time-off regulations—rules for scheduling, call-in procedures, and so on.
4. Care of equipment and supplies.
5. Work assignments and insubordination.
6. Honesty—stealing, falsifying records, and the like.

Validity

Since the purposes of formulating rules and regulations are to insure the smooth functioning of the organization and promote objective standards for behavior, it is important to insure that the rules and regulations are reasonable and valid and conform with federal, state, and local legislation.

Rules that are based on personal whim or preferences will, at best, be difficult to enforce. They are likely to be the cause of low morale and high turnover. In extreme cases they may be the subject of a legal contest. It is interesting to note, for instance, the newspaper accounts of the Chicago nurse who was terminated for refusal to wear a cap that she claimed was uncomfortable and unnecessary and interfered with bedside equipment. Even though nursing caps had been traditional at the hospital in question and were specifically required by the dress code of the nursing department, the judge did not see a rational basis for the requirement and ordered the nurse reinstated with back pay.

This case is a classic example of the need to examine rules to insure that they are reasonable, that is, that there is a *reason* that justifies each regulation and substantiates its existence. The circumstances of the individual employer will determine validity. A common need in many offices, for instance, is for support personnel to stagger lunch and rest breaks so that telephones are covered. In a two-person office it would be reasonable and appropriate to have a rule requiring that such breaks be taken at different times. In a five-person office that requirement would be unreasonable; it would be more appropriate to require that breaks be so arranged that at least two employees are present at all times.

In short, the rule of thumb should be to question the reason for each rule. If a rule can be explained as meeting a real need, it probably is justifiable. If not, it should be reexamined with an eye to amending or eliminating it.

In addition, it is necessary to examine rules to insure compliance with federal, state, and local laws regulating payment of wages, civil rights, and other employment-related matters. Legislative requirements are discussed in Chapter 9; for the present, suffice it to say that employer regulations must not be at variance with such laws or the guidelines established by the enforcing agencies. Rules requiring authorization for overtime, for instance, are appropriate and necessary for budget control, but they must be written and enforced in such a way that the letter of the law is obeyed.

Similarly, dress codes and grooming standards have been the subject of EEOC guidelines and court battles. In some cases rules prohibiting long hair on males have been found to be discriminatory on the basis of sex. Regulations concerning ethnic-inspired hair styles also have been the subject of such guidelines. On the other hand, safety and health considerations applicable to employees operating certain kinds of equipment or working around food justify rules requiring employees with hair beyond a certain length to wear hats or hairnets or to wear their hair tied back or pinned up.

Publication and Communication

Naturally, the larger the organization, the more formal will be the method of publicizing and communicating rules. In a very small office verbal relation of regulations during the hiring and orientation processes may suffice. However, even in such a situation it may be helpful to have a typed copy of rules to give to employees, post on a bulletin board, or otherwise make available. While new employees are being informed of rules, it may be sufficient to have a typed list and to initial and date each rule as it is reviewed. The employee might also be asked to sign the sheet after the orientation session so that a signed record of the conversation can be included in the personnel file.

In a larger organization, a more formal approach should be taken. Each employee should receive a typed or printed list of rules. If an employee handbook is used, a section of the handbook should be devoted to rules and regulations, and discussion of that section should be included in the orientation program. It might be advisable to have the employee sign a receipt for the handbook.

In addition to listing the rules, it is helpful to specify the nature of the penalty that can be expected for rule infraction—immediate or eventual discharge. Abuse of clients, for instance, probably should be grounds for immediate termination; tardiness or poor attendance would lead to termination only after warnings and/or counseling.

Enforcement

Rules should be enforceable and should be enforced uniformly throughout the organization so that discrimination and favoritism can be avoided. Moreover, the manner in which rules are enforced must not conflict with the legal and civil rights of employees.

In addition to meeting objective and valid content criteria, rules must be designed with an eye to enforceability. It may be justifiable and necessary, for instance, to include a rule requiring modest dress or general behavior that conforms to accepted social and moral standards. However, to be unrealistically restrictive or unduly specific defeats the purpose of the rule and destroys its credibility. In the era of the miniskirt, for example, some organizations found it necessary to stress dress codes that maintained adequate decorum. However, when some of those institutions tried to establish an acceptable skirt length based on the distance between floor and hemline, most found the results ludicrous both because of the different heights and shapes involved and because of the awkwardness involved in measuring the prescribed distance to insure conformance.

The uniform enforcement of rules is difficult, particularly in multi-department organizations, in which personalities and priorities vary. The problem can be solved partially by emphasizing, in supervisory development programs, the need for appropriate discipline. Beyond that, it is sometimes necessary to establish an organized system of penalties for all supervisors to follow—verbal and written warnings, suspension, and termination. Not only is progressive discipline established by such an approach, but specific penalties are assigned and help contain offenses. For instance, any employee who is absent without leave might automatically be suspended for two, three, or five days depending on how often he had committed the offense. In cases involving termination, it is wise to have the person responsible for the personnel function review the action and documentation before the employee is fired.

The manner in which rules are enforced has come under court scrutiny with respect to possible violation of an employee's civil rights. Broadly speaking, the situation is analogous to the requirement that police officers have "probable cause" to detain or search a suspect. The point is to protect employees from harassment or entrapment. Even when serious infractions have been committed, the courts have ordered that employees be reinstated if termination was based on evidence obtained in a less than straightforward manner.

In one case involving employees fired for possession of drugs, the courts ordered reinstatement because a supervisor had "set up" the employees by evincing interest in purchasing drugs and agreeing to meet them in the company parking lot for that purpose. In another case a termination was upheld when a supervisor saw employees entering an unauthorized area, followed them because of their suspicious behavior, and observed them using drugs. In the first case, entrapment and subterfuge were found to have been involved; in the second the ruling was that the supervisor had acted within his jurisdiction to check on suspicious behavior—probable cause.

Finally, rules cannot be enforced unless they have been publicized to the work force and the employer's intent to enforce them has been made clear. When rules have not been enforced previously, workers must be told prospectively that management is changing its expectations to include observance of the rules. When such an intent has not been made known, the rulings of courts, government agencies, and arbitrators have consistently favored complainants.

DISCIPLINE AND COUNSELING

Discipline is the maintenance of good order, not merely the imposition of penalties; thus it should be regarded as a positive factor in employee relations, an extension of the supervisory and training function. The core of a good discipline program includes systematic controls and a uniform response to infractions of *established and known* rules. Thus discipline is not just a management tool for identifying and correcting problems; it affords protection to employees as well.

As with other aspects of employee relations, the formality and style of discipline programs will vary with the organization. But in every case it is important to structure a system that will provide order and equity for employees and then develop that system into counseling and problem solving.

Discipline

Discipline can be effective only if management follows a consistent and uniform approach throughout the organization. Routinely, discipline should be progressive; conferences and penalties should become more severe with the gravity and frequency of the offense. There are three aspects of discipline to be considered: communications, penalties, and documentation.

COMMUNICATIONS. Discipline can be verbal or written, and it should be transmitted in an appropriate atmosphere. Obviously, supervisors should keep up a constant dialogue with their employees to correct errors, develop skills and performance, and compliment for jobs well done. Occasionally an error or action by an employee calls for a formal confrontation. When it does, the supervisor should be explicit and objective in identifying the problem to the employee and informing the employee how his behavior should be modified. If necessary, the employee should be told that failure to correct his behavior will result in firmer action by the supervisor. If an employee has been late several times or has taken long lunch hours, he might be told that his pay will be docked and/or a notice put into his personnel file if he does not change his ways.

The written reprimand can take several forms. One is a standard form such as the one on page 106. It is particularly useful in a larger organization or one with less sophisticated supervisors.

A formal memo can be written to the employee and a copy of it put in the personnel file or a memo can be written to the personnel file itself. Such a memo should contain the same basic information as the warning notice. Since a written notice often follows a verbal warning, it should document the previous discussion. As with the performance review form, the employee's

---

WARNING NOTICE

Employee's Name _____

Department _____

Problem _____

_____

Corrective steps to be taken _____

_____

_____

Date	Supervisor's Signature
Date	Employee's Signature

---

signature should be obtained; if the employee refuses to sign, a witness should so attest.

Since warnings are necessarily delivered in a conference, it is necessary to insure that the conferences are conducted in a timely and appropriate manner. Ordinarily, the *person* responsible for administering discipline is the immediate supervisor, but the seriousness of the offense, nature of the supervision, and managerial style may be such that an individual with more authority should attend or conduct the disciplinary interview. The inclusion of such an individual is particularly advisable when the offense has been serious or when recurrence of the infraction will result in termination.

Timing is essential to good discipline. Disciplinary measures should be taken as soon as possible after an infraction has occurred. If the response is immediate, so much the better. However, a short delay may be preferable to allow for consultations, a serious consideration of penalties and approach, or even a cooling-off period. As with any interview situation, preparation is essential to success.

It is imperative to use a private *place* to give verbal or written warnings or conduct disciplinary conferences. The formality of the setting can range from a quiet corner to an office situation with seating arranged to emphasize the gravity of the occasion. But employees should never be criticized, corrected, or disciplined in front of their co-workers.

The *manner* in which disciplinary conferences are conducted is extremely important. The key is to state the infraction in objective and specific terms. Personalities and comparisons with other employees should be avoided. Subjective terms like "I," "we," "think," and "feel" weaken discipline and should never be used; only facts should be discussed. If poor performance is the issue, it is best to confront the employee with samples of poor work; in dealing with attendance problems, it is effective to have a list of dates on which the employee was absent or tardy.

Personal opinion of facts or the reactions of other individuals to employee behavior should not be allowed to enter the conversation. Subjectivity is extraneous and diverts attention from the real issue: that events occurred on a specified date or dates. If an employee brings up other issues or people, he should be told that the supervisor will not discuss another employee with him any more than he would discuss him with another employee.

Special reference should be made to discipline problems that involve more than one employee and those that have potential discrimination implications. In both cases extra care must be taken not only to assure fairness but also to preserve an atmosphere that reflects that fairness. In either case it is advisable to have a department head or personnel functionary present as a witness. If the problem involves two or more employees, it is appropriate to interview them both separately and together and to make sure that penalties are announced at the same time to all concerned. Witnesses should be interviewed separately and be assured that their remarks will be confidential. It is imperative to treat all parties equitably. For instance, if one employee strikes another, the question whether the blow was provoked should be explored. If it was, the employees share the responsibility.

PENALTIES. Disciplinary penalties should be compatible with the infraction, be progressive, and be consistent throughout the organization. As previously mentioned, certain infractions should result in immediate termination. That might be true in cases of proven theft, abuse of clients, and fighting in a work area. As long as corroboration and documentation are obtained, dismissal should be immediate and automatic.

In most cases, however, disciplinary situations will involve less serious matters—lateness, abuse of sick time, continuing poor performance, failure to observe call-in procedures, and the like. They call for the progressive system of penalties: verbal warnings, written notices included in the personnel file, suspension or probation, and discharge. Verbal and written warning systems have been discussed above. Suspension may be handled in a similar manner: suspension of 3 days, then 5 days, then 10 days, then termination. Probation calls for the establishment of a specific period of time—30, 60, or 90 days—during which the employee is expected to modify his behavior. The employee must be told specifically that he is on probation, the length of the probationary period, the improvement expected, the assistance he will receive from his supervisor, and that failure to improve will result in termination or demotion.

DOCUMENTATION. The key to any discipline program is proper documentation. Its importance cannot be overemphasized. An objective and timely account of all actions and conversations will avoid future memory lapses or coloration, provide proof of fair play and evidence against subsequent complaints, and accumulate backup for future actions. In a word, it is important not only to be objective but to *appear* objective to the employee and on the record.

Whenever a serious conference is held with an employee, a record of the conversation should be made. An outline of topics to be discussed can be prepared ahead of time, or a synopsis of the discussion can be written afterward. In either case, both the employee and the supervisor should sign the material. An employee should have the right to express disagreement either by adding his comments to the supervisor's synopsis or by submitting his own memo to file. If an employee refuses to sign, a witness should sign a statement that the employee, in his presence, refused to do so. Follow-up conversations, conferences, or corrective steps, probationary conditions, and any other pertinent information also should be documented. Simple notations by the supervisor usually will suffice for a record of follow-up conversation.

In some cases it is advisable to have witnesses corroborate rules infractions, especially if an employee will be able to disclaim an accusation. If a supervisor finds an employee asleep on the job, for example, having another person witness the sleeping worker will provide helpful backup evidence. In unionized organizations it is wise to include a union steward in the group of corroborating witnesses.

Counseling

The counseling interview differs from the disciplinary session in that its primary purpose is to solve a problem by searching for and seeking to correct the root cause rather than warn the employee that he has erred and must change his behavior. Counseling is an in-depth process; and to be successful, it requires a supervisor who is willing to discuss personal matters and an employee willing to help himself. Counseling is often used to assist the employee who has a satisfactory or better employment history but has developed a personal or job-related problem that is affecting his performance.

Counseling can be initiated either by the employee seeking assistance or by a supervisor who has noted a change in an employee's performance, behavior, or work habits. In either case it is the supervisor who will set the tone of the sessions. It is important to establish an atmosphere in which the employee is comfortable, secure, and assured of privacy. As in any interview situation, sufficient time should be budgeted and interruptions avoided. The supervisor should make clear that he is interested in helping the employee and that the conversation will be off the record.

From the outset the problem should be identified or acknowledged frankly—a recent tendency to be late, inattention on the job, frequent errors, or whatever. Although the problem may be apparent, its cause may not be. Questions based on general observations often encourage the employee to seek and discuss the cause of the problem. It might be work-related—a new work schedule, a co-worker, a rearranged department—or it might be caused by personal problems.

A work-related problem often is easier to deal with than a personal one. Because the supervisor will be aware of any recent changes in the company or department, he will be able to pinpoint the time when the problem began and direct his questions accordingly. In some instances the problem can be solved quickly by the supervisor; it may be a question of explaining the reason or necessity for changes in procedure, hiring additional personnel, or providing a perspective from which the employee can view and understand a situation rather than allow himself to be worried by it. Or the discussion may bring to light the need for additional training for the individual employee or others in the department. Personal problems can be more difficult to deal with because the supervisor will be less likely to have any clues to the situation. As with work-related problems, the best technique is to ask questions, be a good listener, explore alternatives, discuss the pro's and con's, and, in short, act as a sounding board.

Whether the problem is caused by a work-related or personal matter, there are general guidelines to follow in dealing with the counseling role.

1. Objectivity. The empathy necessary to the counseling rapport should not destroy objectivity and balance. Even the most sincere individual is capable of stating his problem only as he perceives it. Therefore, it is necessary to concentrate on fact, and not feeling, when listening to or restating a problem—especially when other people are involved. In some instances, objectivity of that kind in itself will help a worker see things from a better perspective.

2. Distance. A counselor should not get embroiled in the problem—particularly a personal problem; neither should he allow the employee to relate the intimate details of his private life. Such a relationship can only lead to embarrassment and later resentment.

3. Acknowledgment of limitations. If a problem calls for professional assistance or more expertise than a counselor can offer, there should be no hesitation in acknowledging that limitation and in advising the employee to seek appropriate assistance. If there is another individual in the organization who can help, the counselor can offer to set up an appointment while assuring the employee that the second person will be just as willing but more able to aid him.

If appropriate assistance must be found outside the organization, advice should be general—the need for a doctor, a lawyer, a bank, or whatever. A supervisor should never make specific referrals, particularly to individuals with whom he has a personal or professional relationship, unless there are unusual and compelling reasons.

4. Financial assistance. A supervisor or counselor should never lend an employee money, suggest specific investments, or give specific financial advice.

5. Realism. Even when an employee has suffered a great loss, he must continue to function on the job. He can be offered sympathy, comfort, and understanding, but making extraordinary accommodations, excusing unacceptable performance, or showing favoritism in the long run will hurt rather than help him. Neither is it possible to make decisions for an employee or live his life for him.

In short, counseling sessions should be conducted informally and should be designed to assist the employee to see problems in objective terms, solve his own problem, or seek appropriate professional aid. In some instances, it may be possible to provide direct assistance: additional training, reassignment, explanations, or even an accommodation to the employee's needs as long as there is no interference with the operations of the organization.

PERSONNEL RECORDS

Like financial and legal records, personnel files are written statements of fact—dates, figures, data—preserved as evidence, supportive documentation, or a history of events. Payroll costs, orderly operations, and the speed with which applicants and employees pursue their "legal rights" provide great inducement to maintain accurate and up-to-date files for current and former employees. The personnel folder should document every aspect of an individual's employment from application to termination. The facts contained in the file will establish qualifications and document interview results, references, and so on; performance reviews will back up wage-and-salary decisions; warnings and interview reports will justify discipline; copies of letters of commendation, diplomas, certificates, and the like will chart development. Initially the personnel file should include the following:

1. Application
2. Résumé
3. Interviewer's comments

4. Reference reports
5. Copies of payroll notification forms
6. Tax forms
7. Copies of licenses and/or certificates or licensure information
8. Medical clearance or history forms
9. Checklists, receipts, and so on
10. Copies of employment agreements, "welcome letters," union enrollment information, and the like
11. Emergency notification information
12. Documentation of any qualifying circumstances, including preemployment counseling to establish attendance or performance standards

During the course of employment, copies of all materials that reflect the employee's status and performance should be added:

1. Performance reviews
2. Copies of all payroll forms
3. Requests for time off
4. Copies of certificates, diplomas, and course completions earned during employment
5. Warnings and discipline notices
6. Written grievances and replies to them
7. Letters of commendation
8. Copies of incident and accident reports
9. Doctors' statements regarding sick leave, injuries and physical limitations, or ability to work
10. Termination notices
11. Letters of resignation
12. Termination checklist

Checklists have been mentioned twice; they are merely lists of the various forms and procedures that serve to insure that processing is complete. The induction checklist might include application, references, tax forms, insurance enrollment forms, payroll forms, and orientation schedules; the termination checklist should include such items as key and identification return, address confirmation (for W-2 mailings), and insurance conversion.

For maximum efficiency all materials on file, with the most recent additions on top, should be fastened together with a pronged paper fastener. Files should be kept alphabetically in a central area, preferably in the department of the personnel functionary. They should be locked when untended. Because personnel files contain highly confidential information, access to them should be limited to those with legitimate authority—supervisors, department heads, personnel department employees, top management. In most cases records should not be removed from the personnel area. A checkout system might be desirable so the files can be located immediately.

The personnel folder should be used. It should be consulted when an employee's eligibility for promotion or transfer is to be determined, when performance and development from one review period to another are analyzed and compared, and whenever serious discipline measures are being considered.

In addition to the personnel folder, it may be helpful, especially in the larger organization, to keep a mini-file. Depending on the size and resources of the organization, it may take the form of a computerized listing, spindle, or index card file containing an alphabetical list of employees along with department, employment dates, current position, and whatever other information will be useful. A supplemental system of that kind can be an invaluable time-saver in answering requests for credit references and employment verification. In larger organizations it will also provide a quick way to locate employees for emergency or administrative purposes.

In addition to current employee files, complete personnel folders should be maintained for terminated employees for several years. They will provide an accurate record of performance for reference purposes and for use in considering former employees for rehire. Again, it may be convenient to use a mini-file system containing basic employment information—dates, title, reason for leaving, eligibility for rehire, performance review summaries, and the like. A summary system of that type can provide quick access to basic information and allow the full records of terminated employees to be kept in a storage area where they will not take up space needed for more current material.

Federal law requires that organizations employing fifteen or more persons must keep, for at least six months (two years for political jurisdictions), any personnel or employment record including applications, records pertaining to hiring, promotion, demotion, transfer, layoff, termination, rates of pay and other forms of compensation, and selection for training or apprenticeship. However, time limits can be extended to 310 days. Therefore, to be safe, the personnel folders as described above must be kept for individuals during their employment and for at least one year thereafter. (See Chapter 9 for a further discussion.)

TIMEKEEPING RECORDS

A good system of recording time is essential for many reasons ranging from bookkeeping accuracy and employee morale to conformance with federal requirements. An organized system of record keeping will include time-worked, time-off, and payroll records.

Time-Worked Records

The Fair Labor Standards Act (see Chapter 9 for a general discussion of the Act) as administered by the Wage and Hour Division of the U.S. Department of Labor details payment and record-keeping requirements which *must* be followed. Although there is no specific requirement as to the form of records and means of recording time, the burden of verifying time records and justifying payment lies with the employer. Employers are required to establish specific policies regarding work schedules, devise a method of recording time, maintain certain data for specific time periods, and enforce policies and systems.

WORK SCHEDULES. The law requires employers to establish and record definite work schedules for all employees, including days and hours to be worked. The Act does not require meal or rest periods; but if employees are not paid for meal breaks, ordinarily 30 minutes or more, they must be free from their duties for that time. Short rest periods, 5 to 20 minutes, must be paid as time worked.*

* *Hours Worked under the Fair Labor Standards Act*, U.S. Department of Labor, Employment Standard Administration, Wage and Hour Division, WH Publication 1344 (revised March, 1976), p. 2.

WORKWEEK. The Act requires the establishment and formal recording of a workweek of seven consecutive 24-hour periods. The workweek can begin and end at any time on any day of the week, such as 12:01 A.M. Monday to 12 midnight Sunday. The worksheet must remain fixed and can be changed only if the change is intended to be permanent and is not meant to evade overtime payments. In computing hours worked for overtime purposes it is necessary to include all hours worked within that workweek. If, for example, an employee works 50 hours one week and 30 hours the next week, he must be paid for 10 hours at the overtime rate for the first week.* There can be one workweek for the entire organization or several workweeks for different employees or groups.

PAY PERIODS AND PAY DAYS. Although workweeks must be established for purposes of computing overtime, it is possible to pay on other than a weekly basis such as biweekly, semimonthly, or monthly. The only requirement is that overtime be computed on the basis of the established workweek. Usually, it is convenient to establish pay periods that end soon enough before the pay day to allow for computing wages and preparing checks. Thus, if pay days are alternate Thursdays, employees might receive on Thursday wages earned during the two-week period ending on the preceding Sunday. Many problems and pay day questions and complaints can be avoided if employees understand the concept and are informed of the correlation between wages received and hours worked.

EMPLOYEE CLASSIFICATIONS. The Act provides that employees who are not exempt from overtime must be paid at a rate of not less than time and one-half for hours worked in excess of 40. It is up to the employer to establish, based on job content, which employees should be considered exempt and which must be paid overtime and to record which occupations are exempt. Failure to meet FLSA criteria for exempt classifications can result in severe financial penalties. (See Chapter 9 for definitions.)

TIME-RECORDING SYSTEMS. The Wage and Hour Division requires that records of work schedules be maintained, that em-

* The only exception to the rule pertains to hospitals and residential health care facilities, which may opt for a 14-day workweek period. If they do, they must pay the overtime rate for time worked over 8 hours on one day, as well as over 80 hours in one pay period.

ployees on fixed work schedules indicate by check marks, initials, signatures, or statements that the schedule was followed, and that in exceptional workweeks the exact hours worked each day be recorded. However, since the burden to prove the accuracy of records lies with the employer, it may be advantageous to go beyond the minimum requirements.

The most accurate and defensible way to record time is the time clock system under which employees punch their own cards. Employees may sign in and out on time cards or a time book (see Figure 13); they should also sign out and in for all unpaid meal breaks. Sometimes employees will arrive and sign in early. If they do not start work until the beginning of a shift, the employer is not required to pay them. However, when there is a discrepancy of more than a few minutes between the recorded time and time worked, a brief note should be made on the time card and initialed by the employee to explain the difference. Failure to maintain adequate documentation or to enforce overtime policies can result in expensive back pay–plus–penalty situations.

PAYROLL NOTIFICATION. A system must be designed to notify payroll personnel how much and on what basis to pay employees. For nonexempt employees, payroll should be notified how many hours the employee worked at his regular wage and how many hours he worked at the overtime rate. For both exempt and nonexempt employees, payroll should be notified when wages are to include time-off payments such as bereavement, sick leave, vacation, or holiday pay. Depending on the size of the organization, the notification can take any form from an interoffice memo to a separate time card for each employee.

PAYROLL AUTHORIZATION. A supervisor should be required to sign payroll notification forms in order to verify times and make sure he is aware of the amount of overtime worked in relation to budget control.

TIME-OFF RECORDS

In addition to providing employees with timely and accurate payment for time worked, it is essential to insure timely and accurate payment for leave. That requires a system of recording time earned and time taken. If it is computerized, a pro-

Figure 13. Time card.

Day	Start time	Time out	Time in	Quit time	Hours worked
Sunday					
Monday					
Tuesday					
Wednesday					
Thursday					
Friday					
Saturday					

Employee Name _____

Department _____

Week ending _____

Regular time _____

Holiday time _____

Vacation time _____

Sick time _____

Other_____ _____

Overtime _____

Total _____

Employee Signature _____ Date _____

Supervisor Signature _____ Date _____

grammed means of providing, on each pay day, an updated statement of time earned and taken by each employee can be incorporated in the program. The information can be printed on the pay stub. In manual record-keeping systems, there should be an index card system or loose-leaf type of logbook in which to record time earned and time taken. Records should be updated periodically, preferably on a monthly basis. The monthly accrual of time earned is calculated by dividing by 12 the amount of time accruable in a year. If, for instance, an employee is eligible for 10 days or 80 hours of vacation, dividing by 12 results in a monthly accrual of 6.666 hours or .8333 of a day. For such an employee 6.666 hours would be added each month to show time earned. Time taken by the employee during the month also should be recorded. The difference between the two figures will be the amount of time currently available to the individual.

Periodic reports should be made to employees to advise them of the status of their time-off benefits, particularly vacation time. The report can be made on a simple form memo (below) or indicated on pay stubs. Although devising and monitoring time-off benefits is a personnel function, payroll is responsible for insuring that payment is made in accordance with policies. Therefore, a system must be worked out to assure that information concerning time off is available to both functions. In the larger organization with computerized reports, that merely requires distributing reports to both departments. In the smaller

		Period Ending _____
Employee _____	Dept. _____	
	SICK LEAVE	VACATION
Time Earned	_____	_____
Time Taken	_____	_____
Time Available	_____	_____

establishment close and conscious cooperation is necessary. On one hand, payroll should receive copies of all time-off reports; on the other, personnel will need to review time-taken records at the close of each pay period.

PAYROLL RECORDS

There are a number of payroll-related records that employers are required to keep under the Fair Labor Standards Act and various tax laws. Under the Fair Labor Standards Act there must be available for inspection a number of items with respect to each employee covered. They include the following:

1. Name in full, as used for social security purposes, and any identifying symbol or number.
2. Home address including zip codes.
3. Sex and occupation.
4. Time of day and day of week on which the workweek begins. (One notation will suffice if the workweek is the same for everyone.)
5. Total wages paid each pay period covered.
6. Date of payment and pay period covered.

For employees subject to the overtime provisions of the Act, additional information must be recorded:

1. Regular hourly rate of pay for any week on which overtime wages are payable.
2. Hours worked each workday and total hours worked each workweek.
3. Total daily or weekly straight-time earnings.
4. Total overtime compensation.
5. Total additions to or deductions from wages paid each pay period. If such additions or deductions are made, a separate account must be kept for each such employee.

In addition, for employees under 19, there must be a record of birth dates. For employees exempt from overtime the basis on which wages are paid—monthly earnings plus fringe benefits, insurance coverage, commissions, and the like—must be recorded.

EMPLOYMENT RECORDS

It is essential to keep documented and accessible employment files including the applications and résumés of everyone who applies to the company, even if no interview was conducted. Interview results should be documented. If an applicant was not interviewed, the reason, such as "no position available" or "will call for appointment," should be noted. Applications can be kept alphabetically or according to occupational groups. The former system is usually more efficient, since it provides quicker access to individual applications. It is helpful to keep an occupational cross-file as discussed in Chapter 2.

As noted earlier in this chapter, Equal Employment Opportunity guidelines specify that applications must be kept for at least six months (two years for political jurisdictions). However, it is advisable to keep them longer for ready reference and in case EEOC time limits are extended. If space is a problem, files may be relocated to a storage area after one year. In an active employment situation new files can be started quarterly or semiannually and the dated files moved to storage areas at appropriate times.

In maintaining employment records, it is important to remember that, if discrimination is alleged, the employer will have the burden of disproving the charge. It is likely that, rather than justify refusal to hire the individual, it will be necessary to prove that policies, procedures, and practices are nondiscriminatory. The applications of all those who applied for the job in question before and after the alleged discriminatory act will be studied. Inability to produce such records will be regarded as defaulting. The most likely consequence will be a decision that the individual be hired with back pay. In addition, an approved affirmative-action program may be required and monitored if EEOC compliance officers find evidence of discriminatory policies or hiring patterns.

6 MOTIVATION

Marketing and advertising executives emphasize the use of motivation research to analyze the factors that influence buying habits so that they can design their sales campaigns accordingly. Management often gives little consideration to analyzing the factors that affect worker productivity. But just as sales goals are more likely to be reached when there is a systematic approach to consumer psychology, so production goals are more attainable when management considers the factors that motivate the workforce.

The management-labor relationship is not based on a one-sided need for employment and income. Rather it is a symbiotic relationship based on mutual need and the opportunity to achieve diverse ends through cooperation. However, it is management that determines the work environment, and it is up to management to motivate the workforce, that is, to provide a stimulus or incentive to produce. That can be done by employing a reward-penalty system in which employees are rewarded, usually by periodic raises, for meeting performance standards and penalized for failing to meet acceptable levels of production. Or motivation can be achieved by adopting a more comprehensive approach with the aim of influencing workers to strive for optimal performance standards.

MOTIVATIONAL FACTORS

Motivation is based on the concept that people strive to fill certain human needs that are common to all. On the other side of the scale are motivational factors that provide a means of satisfying those needs. On a simplistic level, for instance, thirst creates a need to drink; the factor that can fill that need is a glass of water.

In the employment milieu, people work to satisfy physical, social, and egocentric needs. Management can provide workers with an opportunity to meet their own needs by continued employment and the achievement of high performance standards. By pursuing those objectives, employees will be contributing to management's production goals.

Physical Needs

Everyone needs to seek physical survival and gratification—food, shelter, clothing, recreation. Since in the modern economic structure those items tend to be purchased rather than individually produced or bartered for, the obvious corresponding factor is money. However, the need for food, clothing, shelter, and recreation is continuous, and that implies extended needs for job security, personal safety, and protection from loss of income. The motivational economic factors that can be provided by management include the following:

1. Wages that reflect community standards and internal equity.
2. A system of merit increases in which raises are earned by good performance and withheld if performance is substandard.
3. Objective criteria for performance evaluation.
4. Equitable distribution of bonuses, overtime, and other financial rewards.
5. Fair methods of job and shift assignment.
6. Employment policies that protect the worker from arbitrary job loss.
7. Enforcement of safety rules and use of appropriate safety equipment.
8. Employment practices that eliminate favoritism and discrimination.
9. Adequate insurance coverage.
10. Competitive time-off policies, possibly with bonuses for attendance and length of service.

In other words, personnel policies that promote equity, safety, and security help to create a motivational work situation. It is equally important to foster, by thoughtful presentation of policy information, the workers' perception that those policies have been designed for their use and welfare. A system of merit increases, for instance, should be explained so that workers know performance standards and understand that quality performance will be reflected in wage increases.

Social Needs

Man's social needs can be characterized as the need to form and maintain human relationships. Whether those relationships involve family, superiors, or peers, they influence a person's career decisions, goals, and values as he seeks personal acceptance and approval.

The family naturally exerts the strongest influence. The individual's values, goals, interests, drives, and general attitudes are developed by family example and by his efforts, from infancy, to please and win affection within the family unit. His employment decisions are made within the frame of reference his early "conditioning" has provided and in conformance with the family's cultural and personal values. Moreover, family needs and family perception of his job situation have a continuous impact on his attitudes and performance. Hence, the family's reliance on financial productivity may influence a person to continue to work, but family expressions of dissatisfaction with his earnings or treatment by a supervisor may convince him to seek other employment.

From a supervisor, acceptance and approval usually take the form of recognition of performance, assistance, guidance, and fairness both by tangible rewards like raises and promotions and the intangible reinforcement derived from praise, training, accessibility, and expressed interest. The employee seeks those by striving to meet standards for performance and reliability. In some cases the employee-to-supervisor relationship may represent an extension of the authority structure previously experienced within the family unit, which will underscore the individual's need for a positive association.

The opportunity for social communication that is part of the employment milieu is an important part of the individual's job situation. Although most people enjoy popularity and approval, there are varying levels of need and different means of satisfying it. Job-related friendships which extend into leisure activities are common in the boardroom and on the assembly line, but the need for strong personal ties varies with the individual and his interests. People who derive satisfaction from the work itself may be less likely to rely on peer approval and personal relationships. Socially they may be stimulated by the sharing of work experiences or the teamwork effort rather than personal acceptance or friendship. Those who do not receive personal enjoyment from the content of their work or who are less secure in the employment situation may tend to put peer relationships on a more personal basis. The quality of the supervisor-employee relations or labor-management relations also affects peer interactions. Dissatisfaction in those areas breeds an "us against them [or him]" frame of reference that emphasizes personalities and personal relationships.

Motivating factors related to social needs include a company-wide emphasis on good supervisory practices, reward and recognition systems, communications, and orientation. In addition, there should be a balanced approach to employee friendships that provides an outlet for social interaction without a breakdown in discipline.

Egocentric Needs

All people need to satisfy their "selves." Within the framework of their mental and physical capabilities, interests, and experiences, people seek work they know they can do and from which they will receive some kind of enjoyment. The applications are endless—intellectual stimulation, exercising a particular skill, use of physical prowess, interaction with the public or a segment of the public, the physical environment of the job. The point is that some aspect of the job must have an appeal. Beyond that, people must derive a feeling of achievement within the job situation. Accomplishment, growth, progress, learning, or improvement: some positive experience must result from the work.

The motivational tools that correspond to the egocentric need include training, orientation, communications, effective manpower utilization, thoughtful job design, good job assignment techniques, employee involvement in goal-setting, use of accountability systems, establishment of personnel development programs, and promotion-from-within policies.

THE INDIVIDUAL EMPLOYEE

There are three keys to the successful motivation of individuals. The first is the realization that, despite the generalizations and commonalities of human need, the individual is a unique and complex combination of needs, experiences, and reactions. The second is a perception of the employee as the product of his own experiences rather than someone who shares one's own values. The third is caution against placing undue emphasis on any one motivating factor.

Individual Values

It has been said that the important thing is not what people are but what they want to be. What an individual consciously or unconsciously seeks in his work and how his work contributes to his self-image or will help him attain his desired ends are indices to his motivational needs. Depending on his experiences and the values he has formed, a person can see work as a means of achieving many ends or satisfying personal goals. Some of the factors that may influence an individual are the following:

1. Money. Intrinsic values or current financial pressures often lead people to put a premium on income. In some cases, individuals who have been brought up in deprived circumstances may make money their first concern. Others may have short- or long-term goals—purchasing a home, educating children, investment programs, expensive hobbies, or early retirement—which require a certain emphasis on income. Large families and unusual expenses such as medical or dental bills also put financial pressure on the individual. Still others may see money as a way of achieving power, luxury, or independence.

2. Security. Some people, perhaps for similar reasons, put a premium on job security. Hence some individuals will seek a job in government or in a field or with a company with a history of stability, look for union protection, or even refuse transfers or promotions to higher paying jobs if they feel their job security might be jeopardized in some way.

3. Power. People are attracted to some fields because of the personal power they feel they can attain. That motivation can be manifested in different ways, as by the person who seeks a structured career ladder that will result in a position of influence in a corporation, the politician, or the person who chooses a role, such as doctor, judge, or counselor, in which he will exert a personal influence over individuals.

4. Tradition. Some individuals, out of choice or because of parental pressure, follow family tradition by entering the family business or by pursuing a certain career—a trade, fire or police department, law, or medicine.

5. Glamor. People often perceive as being glamorous positions with high visibility or supposed benefits, prestige, or prerogatives. Hence, there is an attraction to show business, the airlines or hotel industries, personnel, advertising, public relations, receptionist or secretarial jobs, editorial work, banking, and the like.

6. Service. Another emphasis is community service or providing assistance to individuals. This is often sought in areas such as health care, personnel, social work, or consumer advocacy.

7. Mobility. Historically, different ethnic groups have chosen similar ladders to upward social financial mobility. After World War II, for instance, scores of immigrants became busboys and waiters with an eye toward becoming restauranteurs. More recently, other groups have used the education field or civil service jobs.

8. Independence. Some people value a sense of independence or the freedom from close supervision that they seek in their own businesses or franchises, outside sales work, truck driving, or similar occupations.

9. Nature of Work. Ability, aptitude, and sense of enjoyment lead some people to emphasize job content or physical surroundings. Although forest rangers, researchers, racing drivers, jockeys, and all kinds of workers can fit this category, the trait is often seen in those who have clear choices, for instance, those who choose to teach rather than practice a profession because they enjoy teaching so much.

10. Professional Status. A high value often is placed on having a profession, so many people are drawn into medicine, law, accounting, architecture, nursing, and the like.

Whatever the individual's reason for seeking such an end, it is necessary to be aware of his needs and values in order to assist him in developing and achieving his goals.

Assessing the Individual

Whether making long-term plans such as obtaining the educational prerequisites for a professional certification or short-term decisions such as which classified ad to answer, people at all levels of the employment ladder use the same criteria:

1. There is (or will be) a job available.
2. They have a chance to be hired.
3. They can do the work.
4. They will enjoy (some aspects of) the work and/or working conditions.
5. Compensation is reasonable and may be more than the expected starting salaries in comparable positions in another company.
6. Job security.

In short, people are attracted to jobs because, on balance, they anticipate that their experiences will be more positive than negative. The more positive their experiences are, the longer people are apt to continue their employment and the more effort they are likely to exert. The more negative the experiences, the more likely people are to seek new jobs and/or to shirk.

To stimulate employees to high performance, it is necessary to understand the individual and give thoughtful consideration to several questions. What influenced him to pursue his line of work? Why did he apply for his current job? Does he have special financial needs, pressures, and goals? What are his career goals? What about his work does he like or dislike? What does he do best and why? Does he like to learn? How do co-workers regard him? Is he a natural leader? Which "unofficial leader" does he follow and why? Do his goals correlate with his aptitudes? Why does he stay? What is his potential?

It is important to dispel preconceptions about people and their values. For instance, it might be logical to assume that an individual whose position demands more "intellectual" expertise, knowledge, education and/or training would place more of a premium on job content than a blue collar worker would. But the premise of that logic is founded in intellectual bias and neglects the frame of reference of the blue collar worker. Within the individual's scope—his talents, preferences, skills, and the effort required to master a skill—a blue collar worker may be more tuned into job content than a "professional." To a truck driver, electrician, maintenance mechanic, or dishwasher, the content of his job is as important from his own perspective as it is to the physicist, lawyer, auditor, or company president. The point is that people differ in likes, dislikes, intellectual capacities, interests, and ambitions but want to pursue their preferences and interests. That is highlighted by two phenomena: the "drop-outs from the rat race" who sought simpler life styles in the early seventies, and the equalization of wages between many white and blue collar jobs in the same period.*

And it is important to understand the individual employee as a product of contemporary society and his own life experiences. Instant communications and pervasive media impact contemporary society not only by the mass of information and experiences they provide but by their immediacy and graphic nature—live, in the home, and often in color. At once there is a focus on the problems of society—war, crime, terrorism, injustice, population concentration, inflation, pollution, unemployment, and economic instability—a contrast between affluence and poverty, and a highlighting of certain events and people that tends to create heroes and antiheroes. The result is an increased awareness and a constantly developing set of values and "virtues" such as consumerism, safety, conservation, political and social reform, and ecological concern. Those values often are reinforced in the classroom, in which participation and social interaction have replaced traditional discipline and structure.

Equally important is the influence of the individual life experiences. The interests, circumstances, and values of the family and immediate community have a tremendous impact on the development and values—social, moral, intellectual, and financial. The interests and priorities which people see from childhood, the employment of elders and attitudes toward work,

---

* In 1977 unionized supermarket clerks in Chicago signed a contract for more than $11 per hour; assistant professors at a prominent university started at about $13 per hour; starting salaries for registered nurses were close to $6 hourly.

whether there has been approval from family and peers, what merited approval, disapproval, respect or contempt, whether there was stress on achievement—all have a bearing on the kinds of work people do or qualify themselves to do, and all affect the kind of recognition and support people will require on the job. That is not to say people will be carbon copies of those they encounter; it is merely to observe that people will be influenced by and must be understood in the context of those experiences.

Motivating the Individual

Within the framework provided by management, workers must receive both personal stimulation to achieve and continuous reinforcement. Normally, that is the responsibility of the supervisor, who not only is accountable for production but also is the authority figure with the closest and greatest employee contact. Supervisory motivational efforts revolve around five activities: role orientation, training, performance improvement, policy implementation, guidance, and counseling.

ROLE ORIENTATION. Individuals need to identify with the whole organization and to feel important. Therefore, it is essential that each worker understand the function of the entire organization, the relations between his department and others, and the significance of his job. He must be made to feel that his job and the way he does it make a difference to the client, his co-workers, the end product, and the overall function.

The motivational rationale of role orientation is simple. The person who feels his job is important is more likely to exert himself than the person who feels he makes no difference. The role orientation technique, which merely reinforces the links in the proverbial chain, can be employed in every setting: the person who operates the sterilizer for surgical instruments, the sales clerk who assists (or loses) the retail customer, the restaurant dishwasher who insures that sanitary standards are met, the mail clerk who makes sure tax returns are posted by the deadline, the assembly line worker on whose accuracy the safety of the automobile driver depends.

TRAINING. Whether it involves basic skill training, indoctrinating a new worker into methods and routine, or increasing an employee's skills and abilities, the training process is a large factor in employee motivation. Adequate instruction and practice time to master new skills are important to develop the worker's sense of achievement and self-esteem as well as his ability. Workers should be allowed to assume independence at their own pace, but there should be a definite system for checking work, reinforcing training, and answering questions. Good training procedures not only affect production but also establish the basis for a dialogue between supervisor and employee. In addition, workers who are selected for advanced training or who are encouraged to develop knowledge and skills from outside sources receive a tangible recognition of achievement that contributes to their self-esteem and status among friends and family.

PERFORMANCE IMPROVEMENT. The improvement of worker performance should be a daily supervisory function, and not merely part of a periodic review. The supervisor should approach the problem analytically and constructively with the aim of not only correcting shortcomings but adding to a worker's skills and potential. In other words, workers should not only be corrected when they make mistakes but should be helped to do their jobs *better* and to learn new skills. That requires the supervisor to offer specific suggestions for employees to follow and to participate in the improvement process by providing additional training, counseling, or closer supervision. Of course, any criticism must be objective and constructive, and care must be taken to recognize achievement. Employees who know that a supervisor is interested enough in their progress to make a personal effort in their behalf are likely to respond positively.

POLICY IMPLEMENTATION. Policies must be implemented positively and fairly. Effective enforcement of policies and rules requires the supervisor's active support. The supervisor who presents a policy as having been handed down from "them" so that "we" have to follow it not only promotes worker dissatisfaction with the policy itself but has a negative effect on worker morale in general. In addition, the supervisor must take care to enforce policies evenhandedly and show neither favoritism nor discrimination.

DISCIPLINE, COUNSELING, AND GUIDANCE. The maintenance of good order and willingness to assist employees are powerful motivations. Consistent enforcement of organizational regulations adds to employee security by eliminating arbitrary practices, advertising the ground rules, and creating uniform expectations and standards of behavior. Counseling employees to help them solve work-related problems or guiding them to appropriate resources for personal difficulties demonstrates a genuine concern for their human needs. A problem-solving approach to performance or behavioral dysfunctions rather than criticism will be a positive factor in building morale. Career guidance will provide performance incentive as well as growth opportunities for the individual.

MANAGEMENT PRACTICES

Motivation programs can be effective only if top management creates the mechanism and atmosphere which permit the machinery to run. Top management creates the management style followed throughout the organization, sets policies, establishes communication networks, plans physical areas, and sets guidelines for personnel development. Without top management's attention to such matters, even the most skilled supervisor will be hampered in efforts to stimulate employees.

Management Styles

There are two basic management philosophies which determine the style of management within the organization. The first is based on the premise that the workforce is essentially comprised of shirkers who are unresponsive to organizational needs and who require close supervision and control; the second is based on the premise that the workforce is comprised of responsible people who will answer to organizational needs and motivational stimuli and, therefore, will produce in an atmosphere in which responsibility is delegated.

The more autocratic approach obviously involves top management in greater detail in more of the day-to-day activity of the organization. It also places less emphasis on the roles of middle management and supervisory personnel. As a result there are two dangers. Top management might become so deeply involved in detail that it will have insufficient time to pursue broad-range activities such as long-term planning and development, and the more capable and creative employees, particularly in middle management ranks, may feel stifled or overly restricted. The emphasis in the more delegatory management style must be on the employment and development of highly qualified personnel, again particularly as middle managers and supervisors, and the establishment of effective systems and guidelines as control mechanisms.

In addition to delegating responsibility and emphasizing individual accountability, adherents of the more liberal management style might practice "participatory management." That is merely a system under which the employee's role in the planning and/or scheduling process is expanded to increase job interest and involvement and secure employee commitment to reaching production goals. Reduced to simplistic terms, participatory management involves the presentation to a worker or group of workers of a problem, goal, or set of alternative goals and, to an appropriate extent, soliciting assistance in setting up a protocol of some kind. The application, to managers, professionals, clerical employees, or service workers, can be as simple or complex as the situation demands. The subject matter, amount of responsibility, and intellectual complexity will differ, but the principle will remain the same.

In the case of long-range planning or expansion, acquisitions, changes in manufacturing procedures, policy making, and the like, management personnel will be called on to assist in setting up procedures and deadlines, anticipating and solving problems, and the like. On another level participation may mean assigning a porter to strip and wax a specified floor area and having him help plan which area should be done first, what size machine should be used, and a time by which the job will be finished. The point is to get people involved in their jobs and committed to meeting goals in a specified period of time.

Personnel Programs

Although the formation and dissemination of personnel policies has been discussed in another chapter, it is appropriate to highlight their influence on worker motivation and morale.

BASIC POLICIES. It is essential to develop comprehensive policies prospectively so that there is an established framework for employee relations (see Chapter 5). If the workforce senses that management merely reacts to situations, there are two potential problems. First, there is the possibility that the resulting air of disorganization will permeate into production activities.

Second, employees may try to take advantage of the "fire-fighting" approach by forcing personnel issues like wages, disciplinary situations, or job assignments.

Policies should be well thought out, and consideration should be given to their impact on employee morale, production needs, and presentation to the workforce. All policies should be reasonable and justifiable; that is, they must contribute in some way to good order, and the reasons behind them should be explainable. To provide optimal motivational results, policies should provide incentives to encourage performance and longevity. Wage and salary programs, for instance, should recognize and reward good performance; benefit programs should provide security; time-off policies should recognize length of service.

Ideally, policies should be developed before the workforce is hired. If policies are changed or replaced, it is essential to explain them to the workforce and to establish a definite date for their implementation and enforcement. If standing policies have not been enforced, employees should receive prior notice that requirements have been changed. Failure to follow those guidelines will create the confusion that comes when people are not aware of management expectations. The mistake may also prove to be costly, since union arbitrators, wage-and-hour appeal personnel, and similar officials have consistently ruled in favor of complaining employees when rules, changes, and expectations have not been communicated clearly to workers or when enforcement has been inconsistent.

One other point should be stressed. Beyond the formation and communication of rules and personnel policies, there must be uniform enforcement. That means the rules must apply to all departments and all personnel without favoritism or discrimination.

RECOGNITION PROGRAMS. Since recognition of achievement is a powerful motivating force, many companies have developed special programs to recognize individual achievement or provide specific production incentives. The effectiveness of any such program will vary with the size and kind of organization involved, and there is much room for creativity and personalization in developing and implementing any such system.

There are many ways to single out individual employees. Length of service can be recognized with a pin, gift, or bonus for completion of 5, 10, 15 years of service, and the award can become more valuable for those with longer service. In conjunction with that kind of program, some employers have an annual award ceremony or banquet to honor the recipients, or at least provide a public setting for the event. Others prefer to have a supervisor or department head present the award, perhaps in an informal group setting.

Often, employees will be singled out for outstanding performance by being named employee of the month or year, outstanding doorman of the year, production assistant of the month, or whatever. An award of that kind can be conferred on one of several bases: objective statistics, such as completion of the greatest number of production units; supervisory evaluation; or votes by co-workers or even clients. Another variation is to make the award to a group of employees; for example, to the manufacturing shift or line with the best production record of the week or month.

Still another incentive program is to offer a prize to the highest producer, a common practice in sales organizations. Often there are "clubs" for those who sell a certain dollar volume—the Millionaire's Club, Century Club, or the like. In other cases prizes, trips, or bonuses are offered to the best producers or to winners of contests held to encourage production during a specified period.

Occasionally certain occupational groups are singled out for recognition of their service. During National Nurses' Week or Secretaries' Week, for instance, hospitals or companies will stage a "day" within the organization. Again, there are many possible variations: free lunches in employee cafeterias, individual "lunch treats" by supervisors, greeting cards, or just a company-wide publication of "thanks."

Another technique is to publicize the need for performance in a certain area by conducting a campaign to highlight a particular theme. A service institution, for instance, might emphasize the need for client consideration—patient care in hospitals, customer relations improvement in retail outlets, safety in manufacturing. The thrust in such a program is to develop employee awareness and to make an organization-wide team effort to improve performance or public image. That should be backed up by publicizing the results of the effort by circulating favorable comments from outsiders regarding the overall organization or an individual employee.

Work Areas

The areas in which employees work are important to them and should be given much attention in planning, design, and maintenance. The primary focus should be on safety, followed by efficiency and convenience, maintenance, comfort, and special production-related problems.

Safety is a primary consideration not only because of the impact of governmental legislation (see the discussion of OSHA in Chapter 9) but also because of the personal impact it has on the workforce. Employees who do not feel safe will be handicapped by fear in going through the motions of the job and are likely to feel hostility toward the employer who expects them to work in unsafe conditions. From a motivational standpoint it is effective to go beyond the observance of safety precautions and provision of safety equipment by making an issue of safety. That can be done by emphasizing safety in training sessions and publicizing safety procedures, efforts, and effectiveness.

Employees can be involved by having them participate in safety inspections or by including their representatives on committees. Although such emphasis is more likely to be found in a construction or manufacturing environment or in one of the "hazardous" occupations, it should be carried over into other employment areas as well. The average office, for instance, presents many potential hazards from electric wiring for typewriters and lamps to supplies blocking exit doors, unlocked rest rooms, or unlighted stairwells; in institutional kitchens there are fire hazards around stoves and ventilation ducts, sharp knives and utensils, dishwashers, grinders, or even heavy trays, all of which, if used improperly, can cause serious injuries.

The work area designed for efficiency and convenience will be a real asset. Aside from the obvious fact that a job made easier by a well-planned layout will be done faster and better, the employee who realizes that pains were taken to provide such working conditions is likely to respond to the stimulus. The principle in designing work space is the elimination of unnecessary movement. Thus, within the organization as a whole functions should be located in logical sequence relative to the work flow. Central supply areas, for instance, should be located in areas convenient to receiving docks and with easy access to disbursements routes; if the flow of paperwork is from department A to department B to department C, extra work is created for the employees if department B is situated two floors below departments A and C. Again, failure to plan well in this regard can have severe negative effects on morale. If people think management does not care about efficiency, they are less likely to care about production and are likely to make little effort to compensate.

Work areas should be planned with an eye to employee comfort in terms of ventilation, temperature control, lighting, noise levels, and the like. In addition, decoration and color can be used to provide a definite atmosphere—cheerfulness, serenity, action—which will assist in creating the spirit or decorum that best suits the function involved. Amenities such as music, carpeting, and art also are options that may be desirable and which have appeal for certain types of individuals, both employees and clients.

Whatever functions are being performed, there should be a high emphasis on maintaining the work area and equipment. Since people tend to function best in clean, well-ordered surroundings, within the framework of the occupation and industry, priority should be given to work area maintenance. Needless to say, equipment should be kept in the best possible working order. Aside from the fact that employees cannot be expected to turn out top-quality work on inferior equipment, people who see that management emphasizes maintenance of work areas and equipment will have higher morale and will be motivated to produce and to utilize physical resources with more care.

In certain functions productivity is related directly to the social atmosphere of the work area. Assembly workers or pieceworkers in some industries, for instance, tend to be more productive when work stations are set up to foster conversation and sociability. In some service organizations both workers and clients may be more responsive in a less formal or "homier" setting. On the other hand, comptometer operators, statisticians, and similar personnel may tend to function better in more isolated areas where the emphasis is on preventing distraction. When concentration is intense, it may be helpful to provide areas where people can relax for short breaks in a contrasting atmosphere. The point is to look at the function and create the right atmosphere to fit the shared needs of the personnel in that area.

Communications

Although often taken for granted or overlooked as a motivational force, effective communications can be a powerful management tool; conversely, failures in that area diminish even the best managerial systems, policies, and practices. Reduced to basics, communications permit the interaction of people at work, and therefore must exist in order to channel activity into productivity. Work assignments, information, knowledge, priorities, plans, acceptance, approval, rejection—all are *communicated* in some way.

The term "communication" itself merits thoughtful consideration. Rooted in the Latin *communicare* (to participate, impart), communications can be defined as a giving or exchange of ideas, information, or opinions through a common system of speech, writing, behavior, or other signs. A dissection of the definition highlights some interesting and far-reaching concepts:

GIVING OR EXCHANGE

OF

IDEAS — INFORMATION — OPINIONS

THROUGH A

COMMON SYSTEM

OF

SPEECH — WRITING — BEHAVIOR — OTHER SIGNS

The implications are numerous. Communications are not one-way. The "giving or exchange" denotes an interchange, both transmission and reception, a mutually understood basis of exchange. Concepts, facts, raw data, subjective opinions, reactions, attitudes, emotions—all are communicated either verbally or nonverbally (extraverbally). "Verbal" implies a reliance on words, oral or written—instructions, reports, personal conversations, use of newspapers, television, recordings, CB's, letters, memos, signs, and cartoons. "Nonverbal" includes the use of other "signs" or behavior—gestures, mannerisms, tones of voice, pitch, posture, attentiveness, omissions, casualness or formality of demeanor, and even seating arrangements or the use of amenities.

Translated into the work milieu, the focus can be placed on two types of communications: the dissemination of information by management and upward communications. Within that framework several factors are necessary to the development of effective communications. Top management sets the pace. The importance top executives attach to communicating and their attitudes toward receiving information will filter through the organization. All managers and supervisors must be "sensitized" to listen, observe, and insure "reception"; the various media should be exploited; and communications must be geared to the intended recipients.

INFORMATION DISSEMINATION. A tremendous amount of information must be transmitted to the workforce both officially and in the day-to-day dialogue between supervisor and employee:

1. Policies and rules. The policies and procedures of the institution should be communicated so that employees can develop standards of behavior and appropriate expectations. As often as possible, the rationale behind the policies ought to be explained.

2. Goals. The general goals of the organization and the specific goals of the individual's department should be made known, as well as his place in the overall scheme of things.

3. General information and news. Any developments that are meaningful to the organization or workforce should be communicated—even problems. A new contract, high sales, increased production, comments from satisfied clients—all should be shared. The employees made it possible. If the news is not good, official dissemination will help to dispel the exaggerated tales of impending doom likely to be spun by the rumor mill. Such information should be communicated in the most positive way the circumstances will allow so that employees will be reassured and encouraged to rally.

4. Work assignments. The assignment of work is undoubtedly the most common form of communication, and it is an excellent example of the necessity to insure "reception." Work should be assigned in a clear, concise, complete manner. If necessary,

explicit instructions regarding procedures, methods, and dead-lines should be given. Supervisors should make sure that em-ployees understand instructions by asking specific questions, and not merely "do you understand?"

Whenever possible, the supervisor should be the com-municator. He is the person who has the most frequent employee contact, the person who understands workers best and "speaks their language"; he is the person the workforce is most likely to approach for guidance or assistance. In addition, using him as communicator will highlight the supervisory role in the organization, contribute to the self-esteem and status of the in-dividual supervisor, and reinforce the image of the supervisor as part of the management team.

Special mention should be made of the use of company publi-cations in disseminating information. Although the technique can be very effective, it is important that it not take on the image of the "company parrot." Again, the question is that of gearing the communication to the audience. The information, stories, news items, cartoons, and so on should be designed to interest the workers. One way to insure worker interest is to solicit employee opinion in designing the format and employee contri-butions to the reporting or feature articles. It is a mistake to try to slant information, whitewash management, or propagandize in any way. Only if the approach is truthful and straightforward will the material be believed.

UPWARD COMMUNICATION. Providing an employee forum can be a powerful factor in motivating employees and increasing workforce morale. Workers who feel that management is willing to listen to their questions, reactions, suggestions, and gripes will feel like important members of the organization and will be less likely to seek outside spokesmen such as unions or government agencies. An added benefit is the increased information and feedback about production matters that managers will get from the people who perform production tasks. Essentially there are three communications systems that can be utilized to provide employees with a mechanism for upward communication: supervisory dialogues, suggestion plans, and grievance proce-dures.

Supervisory dialogues provide an ongoing interaction be-tween employees and the supervisors with whom they have the closest and most frequent contact. Therefore, supervisors must be trained to listen to employees with interest and discernment and, even more important, to encourage employees to ask questions and to call their attention to problems. In turn, of course, the supervisors must report problems and potential problems to their own superiors. The key here is to advertise accessibility and interest by checking frequently on production progress with individual employees, asking specific questions, exploring alternatives, helping to solve production difficulties, and explaining both procedures and the rationale behind them.

Suggestion plans are a common way to encourage employee communications. Under such a system an employee, possibly with the assistance of his supervisor, suggests a change of procedure to increase efficiency or output. In most cases, the employee whose suggestion is implemented is rewarded financially in proportion to the savings or increased profits that are anticipated as a result of his suggestion. In instituting any suggestion plan, it is essential to follow certain guidelines:

1. Establish a review committee with adequate scope to evaluate all suggestions.
2. Acknowledge a suggestion immediately and inform the individual of the review committee's next meeting date.
3. Hold reasonably frequent meetings.
4. Explain rejections.
5. Establish equitable awards.
6. Publicize the plan and all awards.

In most cases supervisory personnel are excluded from eligibility for such awards.

Grievance procedures constitute a protocol for employees to follow in airing their complaints. Usually employees are directed to go to their immediate supervisors first but to consult progressively higher authorities if they are not satisfied. Typically a grievance system would follow the pattern shown in the box.

In union setups, stewards normally are permitted to assist the grievant; in nonunion setups, one other employee may be allowed to do so. Grievants usually are allowed to submit their problem either orally or in writing. The point is to provide a review system so that employees will feel that their complaints

SUPERVISOR
if no satisfactory answer
in five working days

↓

DEPARTMENT HEAD
if no satisfactory answer
in five working days

↓

DIVISION HEAD
if no satisfactory answer
in five working days

↓

PERSONNEL DIRECTOR
or
GRIEVANCE COMMITTEE
if unable to answer satisfactorily

↓

CHIEF OFFICER OF ORGANIZATION

are heard. It is notable that very often a grievance is the result of a misunderstanding or lack of previous communications; many times a simple explanation or clarification will settle the problem with dispatch.

Development Programs

The aim of personal development is the stimulation of employee interest, achievement, and productivity by increasing the skills, abilities, and potential of the workforce, offering advancement opportunities, overcoming job monotony, and fostering employee commitment. There are a number of personnel programs which frequently are used in the pursuit of those aims: job enrichment or expansion, job rotation and/or cross-training, promotion from within, and accountability programs.

JOB ENRICHMENT OR EXPANSION. By increasing the amount of responsibility exercised by an individual (enrichment) or adding to a person's duties (expansion), it is possible to add job interest and recognize worker ability and achievement. Depending on the size of the organization and the individual circumstances, either approach can be implemented on a number of levels from singling out an exceptional worker to designing a formal program.

Job enrichment, for example, can be as simple as using a good worker to assist in training a new employee (the buddy system) or having a secretary compose routine correspondence or proofread and sign certain letters. On the other hand, it can be developed into a sophisticated system under which a worker is expected to increase his skills within specified intervals and assume more independence and responsibility accordingly. This may involve less stringent supervision of work, an increase in the complexity of assignments, inclusion in decision making at various levels, and progressive responsibility for training and supervising others. This approach is the basis for the levels frequently used to categorize jobs in some large corporations and also in the civil service system.

Job expansion involves a more clear-cut addition of duties such as setting up a machine as well as operating it, performing minor repairs, and conducting inspections. The idea is to recognize the worker who performs well and who has the ability and desire to increase job diversity and his own productivity. Again, that might be as simple as having a comptometer operator assist in preparing the payroll twice a month or as complex as giving a manager responsibility for an additional function.

In utilizing job enrichment or expansion programs it is essential to maintain a concern for wage-and-salary program ramifications. Since it is possible to enrich or expand a position until the job should be reclassified into a higher salary grade, such possibilities should be considered prospectively. If the increase in productivity warrants such action and the additional expense is affordable, allowances should be made in the budget. If not, then the program should be controlled so that the job is kept in the lower salary classification. Failure to do so will counteract any motivational gain and, particularly in unionized organizations, might cause a serious problem.

JOB ROTATION AND CROSS-TRAINING. These techniques of job rotation and cross-training are used to provide additional variety for the worker. Job rotation involves a programmed system in which individuals or groups of workers trade jobs on a regular basis to counteract monotony. Although the practice is probably most common in assembly line situations in which job monotony can be a hazard as well as a motivational problem, it can be applied in many other areas with little or no additional training or expense. Clerical personnel who service clients in certain geographical areas or specified alphabetical groups can switch; kitchen workers can be rotated from food preparation to food service; sales clerks can be assigned to different counters or departments; order-takers can rotate from mail to phone areas; and there are many other possibilities. It is important to rotate people in jobs within the same salary groups so that no compensation difficulties can arise and to employ a systematic approach which will not be disruptive.

Cross-training is usually confined to jobs within the same department or under the same supervisor. It simply means that, once an individual has mastered his own job, he learns the duties, or some of the duties, of his co-worker(s). A number of things are thereby accomplished. The employee's knowledge of his own function and the function of the department as a whole is increased; an opportunity for the employee to increase his skills is provided; a situation in which employees can help one another is established and team spirit is increased (and costs for overtime and extra help decreased); and in-house backup for absences and time-off situations is provided.

PROMOTIONAL POLICIES. Too often "promotion from within" is a phrase in an employee handbook. Few things are as demoralizing to employees as having new employees consistently hired into higher-ranked positions with no apparent consideration having been given to promoting someone within the organization. Therefore, it is wise to establish and publicize a system for opening promotional opportunities to the workforce.

One simple way to provide such opportunities is to post a list of vacancies with a brief list of duties and specifications. Any interested employee can apply for the promotion. His qualifications and employment record will be reviewed, and, if warranted, an interview will be conducted by the personnel functionary or interested department head. Employees applying for such advancement should be treated with the same standards and courtesy as are used in dealing with outside applicants (see Chapter 2). For example, those who clearly are not qualified for consideration or who are rejected should be informed of the reason.

Employers with sufficient resources often find it helpful to establish a "skills bank" to keep track of employees who possess predictably needed training or those who take special courses or training during employment to equip themselves for jobs on a higher level. Still other employers regularly ask supervisors and managers to suggest people for promotion or to assess the promotability of their staff members.

Key to any promotional policy is publication and explanation to the workforce. Periodic studies of turnover statistics to review how jobs are filled, how many employees are leaving for better jobs, how many people were considered for promotion into specific jobs, and similar analyses will provide a good critique of the workability and implementation of any such program.

ACCOUNTABILITY. Establishing in the employee's own mind his responsibility to attain a specific work goal and securing his commitment in effect make *him* accountable to meet his objectives. There must be a mutual understanding of the work objective, work standards, and time frame as well as some kind of commitment on the worker's part.

The application of this principle can be quite simple. For instance, if there is a certain floor area that must be stripped and cleaned by a certain time, the supervisor should assign the work by stating the objective and deadline for completion. If possible, even if it requires a good deal of "leading," the worker should participate in the planning—which side should be done first, where caution signs should be placed, whether furniture should be moved—should be told who to call for help if a problem arises, and should be given an opportunity to commit himself to the parameters of the assignment even if, under questioning, he merely agrees that he can do the job.

Whereas the worker described in the preceding paragraph did little more than accept a prescribed goal and timetable, employee involvement in a process can be extended so that workers have varying amounts of input in the planning process. A typist, for instance, can be asked when a certain job can be finished; a high-level clerical person can assist in planning a protocol for a special project and suggest ways of amending schedules to accommodate the additional workload. Responsibility and accountability can progress through management-level positions and could evolve into a management-by-objectives type of approach.

The focus is not on abdicating supervisory responsibility for directing work, but on establishing, in his own mind, the worker's accountability for completing a goal to which he has agreed. The worker for whom such accountability has been established is more likely to reach a goal than one who is merely directed to perform a set task. Conversely, since goals and parameters are clearly defined and accepted, the worker who fails to attain an objective has painted himself into the well-known corner and can be criticized with greater objectivity. There is a concurrent obligation on the superior's part to allow that employee to reach the stated goal without unnecessary interruption and diversion. If other tasks should assume higher priorities, goals must be adjusted accordingly. An employee cannot be held accountable for accomplishing an objective if he is kept from pursuing it.

CAREER PLANNING. The employee with obvious advancement potential should be encouraged. A counseling session in which the employee is given the opportunity to express his own ideas about what he would like to do and what his ambitions are might be initiated. Some individuals will be surprised to be considered promotable or have not given specific thought to the future. Others may have seen themselves in one role without realizing that alternatives are available.

The initial role of the supervisor is to point out the alternatives and provide advice (or referral to another source of advice) concerning how the employee can best prepare himself for promotion. That may involve new assignments within the department, possible transfer within the organization, acquisition of new skills, or additional education outside the employment situation. It is important, however, not to impose one's own views or aspirations on employees who simply may have different values or likes and dislikes. It may be natural, for instance, for the employment manager to see a receptionist or secretary as a potential interviewer; but the employee may prefer to develop secretarial skills, statistical talents, or just get away from public contact. The point is to provide encouragement, information, and opportunity but not interfere with the employee's choices.

In the case of an exceptional employee a program might be

worked out to establish interim goals and a timetable for the employee to receive specific exposure and training within the organization, perhaps with supplemental education outside, so that eventually he will be equipped to assume a major assignment at a later date.

The purpose of such a development program clearly is to increase worker productivity and worker satisfaction simultaneously. The individual who derives satisfaction from his job because he has a sense of achievement and recognition will tend to be happier and more productive and will tend to stay longer.

7 EFFECTIVE SUPERVISION

As the individual who translates management's plan into action and oversees the day-to-day activities of the organization, the supervisor is key to the success of any operation. Too frequently, however, instead of placing a high priority on supervisory competence and development, management leaves the quality of supervision to chance in both the selection and training processes. There is a tendency to promote a good worker into a supervisory position and expect him to assume his new role with little or no training or assistance. The result is often the loss of a good worker, the addition of a poor supervisor, and less than maximum production.

That need not be the case. Supervisory competence can be pursued and achieved throughout the organization. The development of an effective supervisory staff begins with an examination of the supervisory role and identification of the personal traits needed to fill that role. Selection processes should emphasize supervisory talents and ability, and mechanisms to foster the supervisory role must be established. Finally, supervisors should receive adequate training and support.

THE SUPERVISORY ROLE

In examining the supervisory role, it is important to isolate the principles of supervision from the nature of the work involved, the level of supervision to be rendered, and the intellectual capacity of the individual likely to hold the position. Within the world of work there are countless variables in occupations, individual capacity, and responsibility. Within supervision itself five

147

levels can be said to exist: top managers, middle managers, line supervisors, working supervisors, and lead personnel. However, despite the tremendous differences in job content and the amounts and parameters of responsibility, there are two common elements in the supervisory role: managing work and directing people (or production control and employee relations). The principles are constant; differences are a matter of degree.

Production Control

Production control is the planning, coordination, and direction of activities and related influences leading to the timely completion of work of acceptable quality at a reasonable cost. Whether the end product of the organization or function is a manufactured item, clerical output, or personal service, production goals can be measured. The individual responsible for the end product of the work is the supervisor. To discharge that responsibility, he must plan, delegate, inspect, coordinate, and control expenses.

PLANNING. The supervisor's role in the planning process will vary with the position requirements. The lowest-level supervisor will be assigned a work objective or production goal by his immediate superior, and to some extent he must plan how to meet that goal. That may involve making such basic decisions as the order in which tasks should be done, assigning work, and/or communicating plans to subordinates. At higher levels, the supervisor will be required to estimate production capacity, establish goals, set deadlines and priorities, devise work protocols, analyze work efficiency, suggest new methods, participate in budget planning and control, design functions, and establish reporting structures.

WORK ASSIGNMENT. The supervisor must select the individuals best able to perform assignments and must communicate the objectives, methods, performance standards, and deadlines that employees must meet. He must know how closely each worker should be supervised and must establish checkpoints to insure work completion.

QUALITY CONTROL. At the very lowest level, a supervisor must have a clear understanding of work standards and must inspect the product or observe the operations to insure that those standards are met. Such demands increase with the level of supervision and the nature of the process. In some instances a high degree of technical expertise is required and the supervisor must evaluate the product or service and production techniques with an eye to product improvement.

COORDINATION. A considerable number of behind-the-scenes activities may require supervisors to handle administrative detail and deal with people in various levels of authority inside and outside the department or organization. Work activities of individuals, work groups, sections, or departments must be coordinated. Work hours, jobs, equipment use, and maintenance must be scheduled. Supplies and equipment must be ordered. Reports must be completed.

COST CONTROL. Higher-level supervisors may be required to submit or contribute to budget proposals and to assume responsibility for controlling expenditures to conform to budgets. However, even low-level supervisors have a real impact on cost containment because of their involvement in personnel deployment and work direction. Manpower utilization, overtime assignments or approval, use of equipment and supplies, maintenance of safety standards and accident control, work simplification techniques, and general efficiency have a tremendous effect on costs.

Employee Relations

Too frequently, "employee relations" is a term used only to describe the function that bears its name. In fact, employee relations is an ongoing process for which the supervisor bears significant responsibility. The importance of this part of the supervisory function is quite straightforward. Production results from the coordinated efforts of people, and there is a direct relation between the quantity and quality of the work produced and the relationships the supervisor establishes and maintains with the people under his jurisdiction.

EMPLOYMENT. Because the supervisor-employee relationship begins during the employment process, the supervisor must be a factor in employee selection. There should be an effort to match applicant and supervisor in terms of abilities, demands, and work habits. Although responsibility for interviewing and hiring will vary, the supervisor should be included in the process to some degree. At the very least, a serious contender for a job should be introduced to the potential supervisor before an employment offer is made. Higher-level supervisors should interview potential employees and participate in the selection process even if the final decision is made by a higher authority.

TRAINING. Even when experienced personnel are hired or basic skills are taught by an instructor, the supervisor ordinarily has the responsibility to orient new employees into the actual work routine. More often he must provide training in procedures, methods, techniques, and use of equipment. When new production techniques, developments, or equipment necessitate retraining for the entire workforce, the supervisor is likely to do the training himself or participate in the training process. In short, he must evaluate training needs on a sectionwide and individual basis, develop methods, and teach in one-on-one or group situations. In addition, there is a responsibility to assist each subordinate to develop his potential in his current job and prepare for promotion.

PERFORMANCE. It is up to the supervisor either to set objective standards for individual performance or to see that established standards are met. Thus he must maintain a constant dialogue with his staff, correct errors, make suggestions for improvement, and praise work well done. On a more formal basis, he must periodically evaluate the overall performance of each employee against objective standards and review that evaluation with the employee, usually as part of a wage-and-salary program.

MOTIVATION. To maximize production and assist in individual development, the supervisor must be able to motivate the employee to meet high performance standards. That means he must get to know his employees, be sensitive to their needs, note modifications in their behavior or performance, and encourage them to develop their talents and interests to achieve their potential.

DISCIPLINE AND COUNSELING. Unsatisfactory performance, poor attendance, failure to observe rules and regulations, and other inappropriate actions must be corrected. That requires the supervisor to know rules, standards, and disciplinary procedures. At times he will be called upon to look beyond actions to find causes and assist employees in seeking solutions to their problems (see Chapter 5).

MANAGEMENT-LABOR LIAISON. As the individual who transmits

policies and goals to his subordinates, the supervisor is management's spokesman. He must have not only a clear understanding of policies but also the ability to explain the policies to the workforce in a way that will foster acceptance. On the other side of the coin, the supervisor must be able to represent to management the perspectives and needs of the workforce, production problems, and the like, to contribute to problem solving and policy making. When employees present grievances or serious questions, he must play the middleman—objective but willing to listen and seek solutions acceptable to the employee and viable to management.

SUPERVISORY TRAITS

To fill the roles described above, the individual must possess or be able to develop certain personal traits. A number of qualities typically included on supervisory evaluation forms can be listed to illustrate the point:

Job knowledge	Judgment
Technical ability	Ability to delegate
Leadership	Ability to plan and organize
Initiative	Ability to set and meet goals
Accessibility	Adaptability
Objectivity	Sensitivity
Cooperation	Awareness
Communication skills	Fairness
Cost consciousness	Teaching ability
Problem-solving ability	Use of resources
Decision-making ability	Care of equipment
Stability	

This list represents a cross section of characteristics which can be discussed in relation to the supervisory role as described above.

To solve production problems and to control both quantity and quality of production, the supervisor must have an understanding of the jobs that report to him. Likewise, a familiarity with the function and an understanding of the amount of detailed knowledge and skill necessary for the job are needed for him to be able to evaluate performance, explain the job to prospective employees, coordinate with other functions, and set schedules and deadlines. The working supervisor needs to be a superior worker; the supervisor responsible for on-the-job training needs to know every facet of the job he teaches; the supervisor who is removed from such functions needs a more general knowledge of his subordinates' jobs but must be aware of specific objectives as well as general procedures and methods.

Production demands also call for a supervisor who, to the required degree, can meet deadlines, plan and organize work, establish priorities for himself and his staff, and work with a minimum of supervision himself. He must be able to make decisions, adapt to changing circumstances and demands, exercise judgment, work within the limitations of the available physical and human resources, and maintain good working relations with other sections and departments.

With respect to the employees who report to him, the supervisor must strike a delicate balance. He must maintain close enough relationships with his subordinates to be able to assess his subordinates' work and know their work patterns, see variances in work habits and behavior, know what's going on in the section, and create in the workforce a feeling that he is accessible and approachable. At the same time he must maintain a certain distance; the supervisor who socializes with his employees cannot discipline them effectively or maintain an objective perspective. It is essential for him to apply standards impersonally and show neither discrimination nor favoritism; he must listen to questions and grievances, respond logically, know when to refer the matter to superiors, and follow up. A good supervisor will lead rather than command; he will give his employees a sense of participation in the function and achievement of a job well done.

Whether problems are employee-related, technical, or involve interdepartmental coordination, the supervisor must be objective and strive to isolate facts from personalities and issues. He should be able to state problems and mutual goals in factual terms with an eye to solution rather than confrontation.

SELECTION

Supervisory candidates should be selected with special care and with particular emphasis on supervisory qualities and longevity. Whether candidates are outside applicants or current employees being considered for promotion, they must be appraised not only for individual competence within a specific discipline but also for their ability to provide a positive influence over the workforce.

During the employment process, there should be a double focus on the candidate's leadership abilities and on presenting a complete and accurate description of the job. The successful applicant should have demonstrated that he possesses or has the capacity to develop the personal traits discussed above and to see himself as a part or extension of the management team. Moreover, he should possess a supervisory style compatible with the management philosophies and leadership style of the organization as a whole. An individual with a relaxed, delegatory approach is unlikely to fit into or be happy in a highly autocratic organization; a supervisor who emphasizes discipline and penalty systems is likely to have difficulty adapting to a motivation-oriented milieu.

Candidates also should be given a clear understanding of the supervisory responsibilities entailed in the job, including the scope of the function to be directed, the nature of interdepartmental relationships, outside contacts, in some cases budgetary constraints, and any special problems that are likely to confront them. In addition, there should be a frank discussion of reporting relationships, management expectations, long- and short-term goals for the function and organization, the latitudes and limitations of authority and responsibility, and the usual matters of salary, benefits, and the like.

Only if both parties are comfortable with the terms of employment should an offer be made. The importance of mutual understanding and acceptance is a reflection of the impact of supervisors on the workforce. An enthusiastic supervisor comfortable with his role in the organization will transmit his attitudes to his staff; so will the discontented individual. Since the workers tend to identify with management through their immediate supervisors, high turnover among supervisors will be detrimental to morale, production, and staff retention.

SUPERVISORY DEVELOPMENT

Supervisory competence requires an individual who understands his role and place within the organization, who can establish effective relationships with others, who understands the policies and procedures he must follow, and who can plan and direct work. Good supervisors do not just happen. They learn how to supervise either in a training program or because they have been able to assimilate observations and experiences into a workable personal formula. Certainly a training program provides a more structured and controlled learning experience with better-defined scope and intellectualized perceptions.

Training needs will vary with the experience and background of the individual. On the one hand, the new supervisor usually requires extensive training or monitoring either by formal instruction or on a one-on-one basis. On the other hand, the experienced supervisor new in the organization needs at least a comprehensive orientation in order to function effectively.

Role Orientation

The supervisor must have a clear concept of his role *as a supervisor*. It is important that he be made to see himself as the extension of the management team instead of identifying primarily with his workers. Such a management orientation is necessary for effective communication and enforcement of rules and policies as well as for the efficient assignment and direction of work. The first step in training a supervisor is to discuss the role and its implications along the lines described earlier in this chapter.

Especially with new supervisors it is important to effect an evolution away from the task orientation and passive relationships characteristic of the delegatee into a more positive and dynamic role perception that emphasizes the supervisor's responsibility to plan, communicate and enforce policy, train, motivate, discipline, problem-solve, and take the initiative in establishing relationships with superiors, peers, and subordinates. Perceptual cognizance of the role difference should precede training in supervisory methods and techniques in order to maximize the trainee's appreciation of technique and skill training. Reorientation should begin with general discussions of the supervisor's role in areas like the following:

1. Management-labor liaison. Policy administration; communicating, supporting and enforcing policy; contributions to policy making.

2. Planning. Short- and long-term planning; establishing priorities, goals, timetables; anticipating production problems; gauging production capacity of personnel and equipment.

3. Motivation. Assessing the capacity and interests of personnel; assigning and explaining work; exercising leadership skills; encouraging good performance; providing positive feedback to employees; giving constructive criticism; improving performance; assessing developmental needs of subordinates and assisting the subordinates to establish and achieve professional goals.

4. Discipline. Observing the work and on-the-job behavior of personnel; evaluating performance; correcting substandard performance and behavioral variances; following disciplinary procedures; documenting disciplinary actions.

During this first phase of supervisory development it should be made clear that the relationship between the supervisor and his superior is more complex than the normal employee-supervisor situation in which the supervisor delegates and checks work. In addition to the regular meetings or reports established by the superior, the supervisor should be made aware of the need to recognize situations that warrant his superior's immediate attention. Moreover, although it is usually the superior's responsibility to make his expectations clear, the supervisor should be sure he understands those expectations and, if necessary, should initiate a discussion of them. In other words, the supervisor is *accountable* for his section and must learn to anticipate problems and participate in their solution.

The maintenance of good working relations among supervisors is vital to the overall function of the organization. Thus it is important to emphasize the interdependence of the departments and to encourage supervisors to establish a dialogue with their counterparts in other areas, coordinate schedules, share information, and work together to solve mutual problems. The burden of establishing a good relationship with the workforce lies with the supervisor. Because the tone of that relationship is set quickly and because it is difficult, if not impossible, to correct a poor impression, supervisors must be made aware of the need to establish the right posture with their staff. Emphasis should be on maintaining a balance in the relationship—accessibility and sensitivity plus an appropriate distance.

Functional Orientation

An explanation of the structure of organization should be included in supervisory development programs with three goals in mind: to give the individual a greater sense of identification with the organization by increasing his knowledge; to illustrate the relationship between functions; to establish objectivity by creating an initial impression based on the function of other departments or sections rather than the personalities who staff them. That is an excellent way to provide basic information while reinforcing management style and goals.

Both the reporting system of the organization and the production structure should be included in this part of supervisory orientation. It is essential that the supervisor know the reporting hierarchies within his own function and between his department and top management; this information will assist him to establish effective working relationships within the department and to have a frame of reference in his dealings with subordinates. In addition, he must know how his function relates to others, how the functions interface, and what kind of working relationships he must maintain with individuals from other functions. This is best explained by using charts designed to reflect the desired emphasis, for instance, departmental reporting relationships, production, or consumer service. In addition to the type of management reporting charts discussed in Chapter 1, charts can be developed to show chronological production procedures (Figure 14) or the relationships of the various departments to the consumer (Figure 15).

Figure 14. Process-oriented chart.

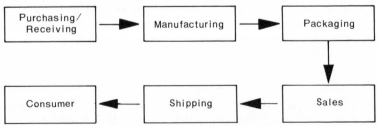

Figure 15. Consumer-oriented chart.

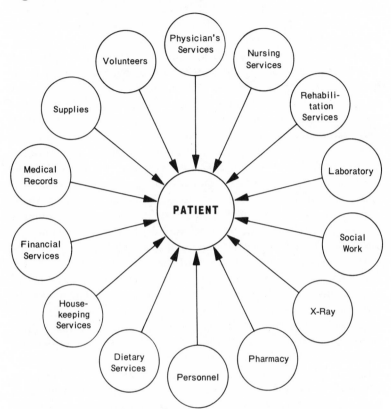

Policies and Procedures

Both in production and employee relations matters, supervisors need to receive a thorough indoctrination in management philosophies, policies, and procedures. Whether that involves study of major policy statements, management objectives, technical manuals, or a general discussion of goals, there must be a framework. Even supervisors who are expected to bring high degrees of functional expertise to their jobs must know what is there and how and why the function or organization evolved as it did. Within the individual level of responsibility are specific procedures including ordering processes, control mechanisms, approval systems, standards establishment, committee interface, information systems, payroll procedures, record-keeping systems, and budget and expense controls. The supervisor will have to administer the policies, follow the procedures, and in some instances improve and improvise. Without a basic understanding he will be severely handicapped.

With respect to employee relations matters, administrative procedures such as processing employment regulations and terminations, status changes, and position requisition forms should be established. A thorough indoctrination on the wage-and-salary program should be given. Particular emphasis should be put on performance review standards and evaluation forms and salary increase systems, as well as a general orientation in the job description and evaluation process. The supervisor will need to know the benefit structure of the organization since employees are to consult him for clarification of eligibility and coverage. In addition, he will need to know sources for employee assistance within the organization—training, benefit administration, health service, and the like.

On the other side of the employee relations coin are rules, regulations, and discipline procedures. This should be a specific area of concern in supervisor training so that there will be equitable enforcement throughout the organization. Since the supervisor will have to support as well as enforce personnel policies and rules, he must know the policies and rules and understand the rationale behind them. Grounds for dismissal, verbal and written warning systems, and "fail-safe" systems must be explained.

Call-in procedures, time-off policies, approval mechanisms, timekeeping methods, employment and affirmative-action obligations and policies are part of the day-to-day process of employee relations. The supervisor must have substantial information regarding them.

Supervisory Techniques

Supervisory effectiveness is a reflection both of what is accomplished and how it is done. Development programs should stress the necessity for balance in each area of involvement. Supervisory techniques can be taught by topics.

PLANNING. The supervisor's involvement in production planning will vary with his level. However, even the lowest-level supervisor should receive some instruction in planning his own work schedules and scheduling the work of his subordinates on a daily or weekly basis. Such a lower-level supervisor can be trained to prepare daily "laundry lists" of tasks to be accomplished by himself and his subordinates and to assign priorities to those tasks. Short-range planning also can be facilitated by weekly, biweekly, or monthly calendar charts that the supervisor can use to schedule work and keep track of deadlines. Higher-level supervisors might be asked to prepare quarterly or semiannual reports projecting the work goals of their sections.

DELEGATION. Effective delegation of work assignments calls for both judgment and discretion. The process can be broken down into steps which the supervisor should follow:

1. Know or ascertain how demanding the task is.
2. Match the ability of the worker with the complexity of the job.
3. Explain the work goal and/or method in as much detail as the worker needs.
4. Make sure the assignee understands the objective, methods, and time constraints and asks specific questions if necessary.
5. Establish checkpoints to determine progress.
6. Inspect or check the final product.

The value of thorough explanation and timely follow-up should be emphasized. The more sophisticated supervisor also should receive training in employee participation in discussions of methods, procedures, and setting deadlines.

WORK ANALYSIS AND SIMPLIFICATION. The supervisor should be trained to analyze the function he supervises in order to increase efficiency and better the working conditions of his subordinates. Although that sounds like a very sophisticated concept, even working supervisors should be taught to break down their work in terms of *what* must be done, *who* does it, *when, where,* and *how* it must be done. Whether it is rearranging an assembly line or mopping floors in a different order, supervisory participation can result in considerably increased efficiency and savings for the employer. There will be additional benefits in terms of motivating the supervisor, increasing his self-esteem, and reinforcing his management orientation.

INTERVIEW SKILLS. As discussed in preceding chapters, interviews must be conducted for purposes of employment, discipline, grievances, counseling, and performance review. The supervisor's involvement in those areas will vary with the level; training should reflect that responsibility. It is essential that supervisors who interview be well trained in techniques as well as the company's obligation with respect to civil rights legislation. Mistakes in those areas can be expensive in terms of recruiting and training costs, production loss, penalties, and unemployment compensation expenditures.

MOTIVATION. To a large extent the supervisor's production effectiveness is measured by his ability to motivate his employees—the producers—according to the principles discussed in Chapter 6. Therefore, special emphasis should be placed on teaching motivational concepts and techniques including:

1. Consistency, timeliness, and directness—an ongoing dialogue established by the supervisor to give and receive feedback on work progress, problems, and performance.
2. A constructive approach to criticism with prompt and direct correction of errors and behavior.
3. An understanding of the human needs, drives, and ambitions of the workforce as well as job objectives.
4. A concentration on actions, not personalities, in discipline situations; absence of discrimination and favoritism.
5. Accessibility to employees and an interest in employee job-related problems and individual development.

Supervisors should be trained to listen, to hear what is said or left unsaid, and to note tones of voice, mannerisms, and gestures, and to be able to interpret such extraverbal communications. They should also be taught how to communicate effectively with their staff verbally and extraverbally by using appropriate seating arrangements, formal versus informal interviews, and the like.

PROBLEM SOLVING. Training in problem solving should begin by focusing on the necessity to state the problem in objective terms, gather the appropriate data, and examine the components on an individual basis. If, for instance, a client is not receiving service because the responsible department is not being notified of his presence, the problem should not be stated as "Department X does not tell us [department Y] that clients are here," but as "Clients are not being assisted." The next need is to list each step that must be taken to notify department Y as well as all the complicating circumstances that are inherent in the situation. A procedure can then be worked out with the help of department X personnel to build notification into the system. It is important to develop the supervisor's perception that the goal of each department is the same—client service—and that problem solving can be a mutual undertaking. Completeness of data also should be stressed.

DECISION MAKING. The act of making decisions can be taught by training supervisors to state the dilemma, reduce solutions to alternative courses of action, and study the possible results of those actions. This is illustrated in Figure 16, which shows the actions that can be taken with respect to an employee who is chronically late. The point is to train supervisors to make decisions after developing and exploring alternatives and to understand the repercussions that can result from following any given course.

INTERDEPARTMENT COMMUNICATIONS. The importance of formal and informal communications between departments should be stressed. Supervisors should be trained to state situations in factual and objective terms and to isolate problems and personalities. They should be acquainted with any forms or form memos they can use, telephone and intercom systems, and effective telephone techniques. They should be encouraged to communicate with fellow supervisors on an informal basis to keep one another informed on areas of mutual interest.

Allied Skills

In some situations it may be helpful to provide special training in communications skills, report preparation, and techniques for effective use and control of meetings. Training in those areas can be designed to provide basic skills or merely to orient individuals to the systems employed within the organization.

COMMUNICATIONS SKILLS. Training in communications in general should focus on four areas:

Figure 16. Decision-making aid outlining alternative courses of action.

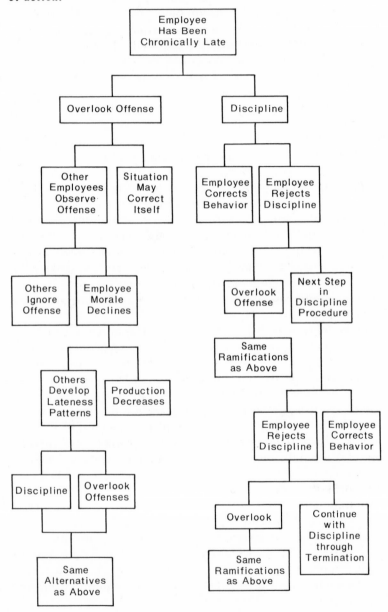

1. The nature and importance of communications: the need for clear transmission, the importance of insuring accurate reception, means of communications, and special communications problems.
2. Techniques: gearing communications to the audience, the act of listening, encouraging others to participate, the importance of upward communications.
3. Receivers of communications: employees, peers, superiors, "publics" including clients, outside contacts, and the general public.
4. Nonverbal communications: how to recognize, read, and use them.

Specific communications systems, including grievance procedures, house publications, staff meetings, and other methods of disseminating information within the organization, should be made part of the orientation or training process, as should companywide techniques for upward communications. Some groups or individuals may need training in oral or written communications, including preparation of material for oral presentation and public speaking skills, business English, composition of letters, reports, proposals, interoffice communications, and the like. It may be necessary to explain communications systems and equipment, including telephone and intercom techniques.

REPORTS. Effective reporting systems are key to the successful operation of any organization. Supervisors need to establish good reporting systems with their subordinates to insure adequate control over the production process and, in turn, be able to report to their own superiors on progress, problems, and general development. The importance of receiving feedback and keeping others informed, as well as formal and informal reporting methods, should be stressed. If formalized reports are required periodically, the format, content, and computation methods may be included as training material.

MEETINGS. The effective use and control of committees and meetings may be a good subject for training. Preparation of agendas, control of time, and rules of procedure are necessary for economical and productive meetings. In addition, the use of meetings and committees as a forum to air new programs and ideas and to secure support is an art from which many supervisors and organizations may profit.

MANAGEMENT SYSTEMS

No matter how able or well trained a supervisor is, he cannot function at optimal efficiency unless top management recognizes and supports the role. That requires an organizational emphasis on creating management systems that highlight the role of supervisor and support the individual. Such a system should include employee relations functions, communications, reporting systems, the opportunity for peer group interactions, and an emphasis on supervisory accountability.

Employee Relations

The employee relations process should feature the supervisor. In order to establish the importance of the role from the prospective employee's first contact with the organization, the supervisor should be included in the interview process in some way and should be given some role in the departmental orientation. As previously discussed, within the frame of fair employment practices the applicant should be screened for compatibility with the supervisor.

The supervisor must have a real and obvious role in the performance reviews and salary decisions. If he does not actually conduct the performance review interview himself, it may be advisable to include him in at least part of the process. The maintenance of good discipline requires the inclusion of the supervisor in disciplinary conferences even when circumstances indicate the dominance of a high authority in the proceedings. As much as possible, the disciplinary prerogatives and decisions of the supervisor should be upheld. The supervisor always should be the first step in grievance or questioning procedures. Even when, in the interest of maintaining his own accessibility, a person higher in the chain of command becomes involved first, the supervisor should be brought into the process unless there is an overriding reason to exclude him.

Communications

If the supervisor is to be effective in his production and employee relations activities, he must be kept informed. The planning of production schedules, overtime schedules, establishment of priorities, work assignments, expenditures, budget control, and related activities must be conducted within the framework of organization and department goals and resources. Therefore, it is essential to keep the supervisor informed of changes in goals or plans, interdepartment developments, and similar issues that may affect production planning and control. Circumstances of that kind might include loss of sales contracts, a shortage of raw material, delay in obtaining supplies, proposed in-house construction, a change in product specifications, and personnel problems or understaffing in other departments.

With respect to his employee relations responsibilities, the supervisor must be able to answer questions about changes and developments both to maintain his own credibility among his subordinates and to help dispel the apprehensions that often are byproducts of the rumor mill. Since he will have to support and enforce personnel policies and regulations, it is particularly important that he be advised of changes in those areas and be kept up to date on labor contracts, union activities, and general labor relations tendencies.

In addition, the supervisor should be utilized to disseminate information to the workforce. That practice will not only increase his own image among his subordinates but also increase the effectiveness of the communication process. Supervisors, being closest to the workers, will be able to present information in a more understandable and acceptable way, and they are more likely to receive honest reaction and feedback. Thus even major announcements appropriately emanating from high authority should be supplemented by supervisory input. (It is interesting to note that the many studies that have been conducted on this topic report worker preference for communications from immediate supervisors.)

Reporting Relationships

An organization-wide effort should be made to design reporting relationships, both structurally and personally, to enhance the supervisory role and support the supervisory staff. Structurally, the reporting hierarchy must be clearly defined and appropriately organized in terms of professional expertise and importance. Thus on the one hand it is essential that supervisors report to one single superior whenever possible. In situations in which responsibilities for a given function are split between two or more individuals, there should be a clear differentiation of authority. For example, if the supervisor of shipping and receiving in a large office is responsible to the office manager for mail pickup and distribution activities and to the purchasing director for supply ordering, receipt, and control, the distinction of authority should be made clear.

On a personal basis, managers should be encouraged to develop close reporting relationships with supervisors and to include them, whenever possible, in planning and reporting sessions with their own superiors and between departments. Thus if a director of purchasing is reporting to a vice president on proposed supply inventory systems, the supervisor of shipping and receiving may be included in the meeting for input and information. This inclusion will reinforce the supervisor's management orientation, improve his self-image, and increase his status among his staff, as well as add to his knowledge and perhaps aid in his development.

Peer Groups

Focusing on supervisors as a group can be an excellent method of highlighting the supervisory role and fostering peer relationships that contribute to intersectional and interdepartmental cooperation. The most common way to accomplish this is to hold periodic meetings of the supervisory staff, perhaps a lunch-hour gathering accompanied by sandwiches and coffee, at which top management or an individual department conducts a briefing to supply supervisors with information on new developments, campaigns, or policies. A new union contract or employee benefit program, a change in financial reporting systems, the implications of newly passed legislation affecting production techniques, product design, safety standards, or employment practices might be topics for such a meeting. The meeting will not only create a peer group experience but also provide an excellent system for supplying information and a forum for feedback or practical discussion of problems and implementation. Moreover, the interdepartmental representation will present an opportunity for supervisors to get an insight into the problems and problem-solving techniques of other disciplines.

In some instances social events, sports outings, or development sessions followed by social periods like lunches, dinners, or coffee breaks may promote the desired peer interaction. An established practice for executives, this technique could be adapted to fit any group.

Accountability

If supervisory competence is to be achieved on an individual and companywide basis, the supervisory role must be stressed to supervisors as well as the workforce, and the former must be held accountable for their performance as supervisors.

Accountability starts with a clear understanding, by individual and superior, of goals and performance standards and requires a joint commitment to attain both objectives and standards on both a short- and a long-term basis. Thus the supervisor should be held accountable for meeting daily, weekly, or monthly production goals and for providing the employee direction and support demanded of the supervisory function. In addition, all supervisory performance evaluations should reflect the supervisory function as well as technical or professional expertise. Such a technique requires emphasis on two factors: what is done and how it is done. Supervisory performance reviews should be specially designed to reflect appropriate criteria such as ability to plan and organize, interdepartmental cooperation, and communication skills. That contrasts with the more general performance factors, like quantity and quality of work, often used for evaluating the workforce.

SUMMARY

A competent supervisory staff is the product of commitment. It requires a determination to select only candidates with talent for supervising and to train supervisors to develop that skill. But in the final analysis, management must, on the one hand, provide an atmosphere in which good supervision can and will flourish and, on the other, require the supervisory staff to channel their energies to fill the role with competence.

8 TRAINING AND DEVELOPMENT

In many organizations training is limited to teaching a new employee tasks, jobs, and routine. Very often the training is conducted extemporaneously with little organization or consideration of goals and technique. With a more organized approach and a wider perspective, even in a small business initial job training can be improved, and additional programs can be implemented to produce a significant impact on production and personnel.

Effective training and development programs can help to improve production by equipping employees with better skills in less time, can contribute to employee motivation and staff stability by increasing job satisfaction and fostering a sense of identification with employer and employment, can produce a growth in employee development to parallel anticipated organization growth, and can facilitate overall adjustment to changes in production techniques and methodology. In addition, when warranted by public relations needs, the training function can reach beyond the organization into community-oriented projects.

Whatever the size or routine of the operation, consideration ought to be given to the benefits that can be derived from the various training activities, as well as the means of developing them. Successful training in any of those areas requires accurate assessment of needs, the development of specific goals, utilization of effective training techniques, program design, and follow-up. In addition, the timeliness of training is important; it is always easier for people to learn fresh material correctly than it is for them to correct poor techniques and relearn job skills.

168

TYPES OF PROGRAMS

For purposes of this discussion, training and development programs can be broken down into five categories: general orientation, job training, development programs, special training, and community-oriented programs. Generally, the need for orientation and job training is universal, and additional program requirements vary with the organization and labor market.

General Orientation

A general orientation to the company is necessary, whether it is done on a one-to-one basis in the small office or in the formal program needed in the larger organization. The purpose of such an orientation is fivefold:

1. To give the new employee an overview of the organization—its goals, structure, and key personnel.
2. To define the new employee's position within the company; to make clear that the newcomer is a part of the whole, has an important function, and is a link in the chain.
3. To tell the new worker what is expected of him as an individual and to acquaint him with rules, regulations, and procedures.
4. To let the employee know what he can expect from the company in terms of benefits, salary reviews, promotional opportunities, and the like.
5. To establish a line of communications between the employee and management.

The informal orientation may be conducted by the personnel functionary, the department head, or an immediate supervisor. However, it is essential to designate an individual with a thorough knowledge of the material to be covered, including benefit information. Even in the one-on-one orientation, "handouts" are helpful; they might include benefit explanations, diagrams of the office with names, a copy of the organization chart, lists of holidays and pay days, synopses of time-off policies, or explanations of unusual or technical jargon or language. The material need not be elaborate; photocopies or mimeographed sheets will suffice.

In the more formal setup, the personnel or training functionary should host the program, which should include remarks by other speakers, including representatives of key departments, benefit specialists, and the like. The use of visual aids, such as charts, slides, and movies, may be helpful, and handouts are a must—handbooks listing rules, regulations, policies, benefit information, and safety and security information. The following outline represents a typical program which could easily be adapted to suit individual needs:

I. Welcome
II. An overview of the organization
   A. History
   B. Present structure
   C. Goals—organizational long- and short-term
   D. Philosophy: service to client,
      quality products, and the like
   E. Key people
III. Policies and procedures
IV. Benefits and employee services
V. Safety and security
VI. Tour of the premises

In short, the new employee should come away from the general orientation with an awareness of the purpose, personality, and structure of the organization, a perception of management's expectations, and specific knowledge of policies, rules, benefits, and the resources available to him.

Job Training

Every employee requires some job training either because of the uniqueness or complexity of the job situation itself or because of a lack of adequate preemployment training. The levels of need will vary, as will the ability of the individual to meet those needs independently and adapt to new situations and techniques. But whether the training involves the executive who uses files, reports, contracts, and conferences to orient himself to the operations of a new job situation or an unskilled worker who needs someone to teach him basic skills, an organized and analytical approach to training is necessary.

In the case of the higher-level employee, care should be taken to make available the materials needed for independent study and research. Meetings and conferences with key people should be arranged, and sufficient time should be scheduled to allow appropriate discussion of problems and interchange of information and views. The program should be structured to reflect both the priorities of the organization and the needs of the individual. It may be appropriate to assign another person on or near the newcomer's level the responsibility for setting up the program and supporting the new employee.

The technical or clerical worker will need more specific guidance, the extent of which will depend on individual background and experience. Specific equipment models, systems, procedures, work schedules, and the like should be explained. A new computer operator, for instance, will need to know the flow of data through the input preparation and key punch areas as well as job schedules, deadlines, some programming techniques, storage systems, control setups, and similar information. In some cases, a familiarization with the computer model will be necessary.

A secretary, at the least, will need to be acquainted with telephone-answering procedures; message systems; dictating, communications, and copy systems; supply areas; company forms; the superior's work schedule, filing system, frequent callers, and frequently called numbers; requisition systems; and possibly technical language. That kind of training requires varying amounts of effort. Much can be manualized and the necessary personal attention reduced for the most part to initial review of material, supplemental information, and follow-up.

Unskilled workers and those hired to fill unique or highly structured jobs will tend to need very specific instruction on equipment usage, work techniques, job schedules, procedures, and the like—in other words, basic skills and job know-how. Training of that kind requires close and consistent teaching and observation with frequent inspection and follow-up.

Job training also may be required to reflect changes within the organization, whether those changes are administrative or technical in nature. A restructuring of reporting relations, new methods or procedures, equipment, machinery or model changes, legislation, policy and contractual changes, and a host of similar developments can trigger training or retraining efforts on various levels and of varying intensity.

Development Programs

In addition to equipping the individual with the skills and knowledge to meet the requirements of his job, training is concerned with increasing employee ability and potential to meet the staffing and production needs of the organization through skill acquisition and personal development.

There are two basic approaches to increasing individual skills. One is directed toward improving the employee's current productivity; the other equips the employee with skills for promotional opportunities. Current productivity can be increased by providing either remedial or advanced training in the work currently assigned to an employee and by adding to skills through cross-training or job enlargement techniques (see Chapter 6). The thrust of such training is to increase individual output by increasing the quantity of work performed. At the same time, the technique may provide substantial motivation and, as a side effect, equip the worker with skills for possible advancement.

In contrast, a program for personal development is designed specifically to increase the employee's skills for his own advancement purposes. The program can consist of specific educational activities such as a stenography course to enable a good typist to advance into a secretarial position, accounting courses for accounting clerks, or management courses to qualify supervisors or middle managers for higher positions. Within the job situation personal development can be achieved in many ways: the assignment of progressively more complex work, the inclusion of a subordinate in meetings and on committees, having a subordinate represent a superior at some meetings, or delegating responsibility for specific projects. Subordinates also can act for the superior in his absence or contribute to goal setting and planning. In other words, superiors can groom individuals for advancement by a gradual and controlled exposure to increased reponsibility and management personnel.

Special Training

The labor market, client population, or organizational priorities may create training needs in specialized areas. For example, in organizations that draw heavily on non-English-speaking populations for employment needs it may pay to offer courses in English as a second language. If the client population is largely foreign, it may be helpful to provide foreign language instruction, even on a limited basis, to improve client-employee communications. General-education courses to allow employees to obtain high-school equivalency diplomas, business writing or business mathematics, and safety training are other examples of such specialized programs. It may be advantageous for some employers to sponsor classes in basic nutrition and sanitary techniques or even stop-smoking clinics. Programs can be developed in any area that will benefit employer and employee.

Community-Oriented Programs

Public relations concerns, civic responsibility, or the need to develop a future labor pool might necessitate the development of community-oriented training programs. Such programs can vary from public tours of the operations to special-education programs for adults and youngsters. Participation in summer employment programs for students or work-release programs in conjunction with local high schools may be beneficial, especially if student salaries are paid through special grant programs.

Attendance at high school or community college "career days" or providing facilities for students to get practical experience under the tutelage of high school or college instructors may be appropriate. Or it may be advantageous to offer refresher courses in specialized areas to community members in order to develop a labor pool to meet chronic employment needs. Hospitals frequently provide such training to nurses who have not practiced recently; there is no reason why similar programs could not be offered to secretaries or other clerical workers with rusty skills. In some instances expenses may be offset by charging nominal fees or by obtaining a federal training grant.

ASSESSMENT OF NEEDS

Training programs should be developed and implemented only if there is a definite and explicit need to be met within the organization. In some cases the needs are obvious, for example, for general orientation, new employee training, and changes in equipment, procedures, and techniques. In others the need for training comes to management's attention when production difficulties emerge. In those instances it is necessary to examine the situation carefully to determine actual rather than apparent need. If production falls in a certain department, for instance, additional employee training might seem to be the logical solution. A careful investigation, however, may reveal the need for supervisory training or uncover a motivational problem. Or there may be a need for better employee selection criteria, equipment maintenance, work-simplification techniques, improved supply distribution, or other work modifications. In short, although training is an effective aid in maintaining production levels, it is not the answer to every production problem.

Not all production difficulties are dramatic enough to alert management that the need for training should be considered. Managers and supervisors have a major role in determining training needs through personal observation. Production reports, analyses of employee relations activities, and employee surveys can call attention to a training need or be used as a tool in determining the specific areas of need and establishing the goals of the training effort.

A supervisor or manager often will be able to determine that a training need exists either for a work unit as a whole or for individuals within the group by observing performance and reviewing the quantity and quality of production. Or he may be able to single out an individual worker for personal development. Even when the determination is made by using other sources, the supervisor or manager should be consulted to help pinpoint the need and the thrust of a potential training effort.

As mentioned above, a drop in production or a decrease in product quality frequently is a symptom that a training need exists. Any production failures should be investigated in that light. Once the decision to proceed with training has been made, it is important to study the production process and employee performance with an eye to determining the particular direction the training effort should take.

Employee relations activities can be important indicators for training in several ways. Consistently poor performance evaluations for the employees of any department or work unit may indicate a need for additional job training, supervisory development, or further explanation of performance review factors or the merit increase system. A pattern of employee grievances may provide a similar warning that training and development programs are in order. Similarly, an examination of turnover statistics, possibly to be complemented with exit interviews, or a review of questionnaires completed by terminating employees, can be an effective indicator. A pattern of short-term employment is a particularly relevant index of training-related turnover problems.

There is one other technique that can be very useful—the employee survey. Like the job questionnaire used in writing job descriptions, the survey form investigatory method can be especially useful because it elicits information from the producers themselves. Questionnaires should be geared to the people who will be asked to complete them (Figure 17). The goal is to obtain straightforward but comprehensive information including what the individual perceives his own training needs to be, as well as those of his co-workers and employees in related work units. Questions should be worded in simple language, and in most instances the forms should be brief. Follow-up interviews can be conducted with employees if necessary. After survey data have been collated, they should be reviewed and discussed with the supervisor or department head.

TRAINING TECHNIQUES

Training can be conducted on a one-on-one basis, in lectures, home study programs, or seminars, or by combining two or more of those approaches. The training methods ought to reflect the number of trainees and their needs as well as the material to be covered.

Whichever method is selected, several principles are constant. Although good training results in improved production, training costs money both in production loss while trainees are being instructed and the expenditure of the trainer's time, particularly if a line supervisor is conducting the session. Therefore, it can be cheaper to train a number of employees at the same time instead of covering the same material in successive one-on-one sessions. Naturally, cost must be balanced by the effectiveness of the method. Training is an investment that should reap higher production yields, and it therefore should be designed to achieve maximum results.

Figure I7. Training questionnaire for support personnel.

Employee Name _____

Job Title _____ Department _____ Start Date _____

---

1. What kind of training did you receive when you started your present position?

   On-the-Job Training ☐   Class ☐   Group Training ☐

   Individual Training ☐   Other – specify _____

2. Who trained you?

   Supervisor ☐   Training Specialist ☐   Other – specify _____

   _____

3. Do you think your job training was

   Poor ☐   Satisfactory ☐   Good ☐

4. Do you think you could do your job better if you received additional training now?

   Yes ☐   No ☐

5. If Yes, what additional training do you think would benefit you?

   _____

6. Do you think others in your work unit would benefit from additional training?

   Yes ☐   No ☐

7. If Yes, what additional training is needed? _____

   _____

8. Do you think employees in other work units would benefit from additional training?

   Yes ☐   No ☐

9. If so, what training? _____

   _____

   _____

Employee Signature _____ Date _____

One-on-One Training

Particularly in the small organization or department in which employees are hired at a slower rate, one-on-one training can be a most effective technique because it allows the trainer to respond to the very individual needs and learning rate of the trainee. Unfortunately, one-on-one training frequently is approached haphazardly. Actually, it should be approached with the same preparation and planning that is devoted to formal lectures.

Key to the one-on-one technique is the presentation of material in digestible units and the provision of "practice time" to allow the employee to master each subject. With that approach there is a unique opportunity to maintain accessibility for trainee questions and to correct errors and poor work habits without costly delay. One-on-one training is often particularly effective if backed up by use of a structured text or operations manual. (See the discussion on course materials later in this chapter.)

As an extension of more structured job training, it is sometimes helpful to employ the buddy system. This one-on-one technique involves the assignment of a senior employee with a good work record and good work habits to assist the trainee during the practice and work periods that are ordinarily interspersed with training sessions. Although the buddy system can be a highly effective supplement to training, it cannot replace higher-level training and should not be expected to do so. It is also important that the senior employee understands his role and his supervisor's expectations and that the areas he is to cover be delineated clearly.

The Lecture

Although it has lost popularity in many educational circles, the lecture or formal classroom approach to training and teaching still is highly effective. When large groups of trainees are involved or when highly technical material must be taught, the lecture provides an excellent opportunity to structure and present the subject with a logical and concise progression of ideas and concepts in an atmosphere that fosters trainee concentration.

The lecture technique does demand a trainer with good public speaking skills, including the ability to hold attention, vary the pace, and create appropriate emphasis within the scope of the subject. A special effort should be made to insure the adequate grasp of the material by the audience and it is important to incorporate into the program an opportunity for trainees to apply the theory or technique. Thus there should be some degree of audience participation either in question-answer periods or "laboratory" sessions in which employees can duplicate the demonstrated technique or apply the theory to practical work situations. Key to successful lecture techniques is the use of audiovisual aids, texts, and other materials to be discussed more fully subsequently.

Home-Study Programs

Although home-study programs have their place in the training function, they should be used with discretion. Essentially, home study is a correspondence course approach in which the trainee is given material to study on his own. There are two difficulties involved: the reliability of the trainee and the lack of trainer availability. The concept of home study presents many variables: the amount of time available to the trainee, the distractions and disruptions of the home environment, and even the tenacity (or lack of it) with which individuals are apt to pursue their studies. If correspondence-type courses must be used for essential training, it is better to make time available to the employee during working hours and to supply a controlled area for the training.

Voluntary education programs, such as general-education programs, are more likely subjects for home study, since they are usually presented as an educational benefit rather than required job-related training. It is important to note that nonexempt employees who are *required* to complete home training as a condition of employment must be paid for that time as time worked (see Chapter 9).

The unavailability of an instructor to answer questions and provide supplementary information on the spot is a serious drawback in even the best-designed home-study programs. Failure to grasp certain concepts accurately can cause a trainee to misconstrue ensuing material even though he might not be aware of the aberration. Frustration at not being able to grasp material can prevent some trainees from completing a program. The emotional response of trainees to such frustrations cannot be compensated by the availability of assistance at a later time; immediacy of response and assistance are important in any learning process.

If home-study courses are used in any capacity, it is advisable to institute deadlines for completion of segments of the course. Tests should be given when those deadlines occur to insure both comprehension of the material and timely completion of the work. It is usually better to administer the tests during working hours as a motivational tool as well as a monitoring device.

Seminars

Seminars have come to be extremely popular. They involve an informal discussion of a given topic by a participative group led by a trainer or discussion leader. Because there is active discussion by all participants, seminars provide a highly motivational and often challenging learning environment. Trainees are required to think not only to grasp basic concepts but to respond to the discussion of those ideas. The stimulus comes not only from the instructor but from the peer group, concerns about image, and self-esteem.

Since seminars are effective only if there is considerable interaction among the group, they should be used only when the number of trainees is limited, up to about ten, and when the group is likely to participate. The participants ordinarily need a certain intellectual sophistication and the ability to articulate, and should have fairly similar backgrounds.

The task of leading a successful seminar is not easy. It demands an individual with a wide knowledge of the subject who can both elicit an even participation from the trainee group and, without dominating, control the discussion so that all the material is covered with appropriate emphasis and perspective. In effect, the leader must structure the discussion to meet the needs of trainees and the demands of the material.

Handouts, role playing, and laboratory periods are effective seminar-managing tools. In addition, the stimulation of response by questioning participants, the creation of practical examples, and strict control of time are necessary. The material covered must be limited enough in scope to allow for comprehensive treatment of the subject within the time frame and broad enough that people can discuss the topic from different perspectives.

Work Simulation

Simulating the work conditions and/or atmosphere is another approach to training. Frequently used to teach mechanical skills, it has the advantage of allowing employees to learn at their own pace without slowing down the production process or interfering with client relations.

The classic example of the simulation technique is the use of nonoperative cash registers to train retail sales personnel. In the isolation of the training area, trainees can practice ringing up sales and validating charge information without delaying customers or using valuable space in the selling area. Another example is the use of mock hospital rooms or volunteer and dummy ("Resuscitation Annie") patients to train nurses' aides or orient registered nurses into hospital routines and systems.

Work simulation techniques can be expensive, since they require the use of a certain amount of nonproductive space and machinery. Recreating an assembly line or other expensive machinery, for instance, involves a considerable investment of capital from which there will be no direct income. However, the level of skills that can be developed, the safety element, and the lack of interference with the production process can justify the expenditure.

A similar technique is used in management development programs, in which "war planning sessions" are held to train managers to react to potentially high pressure business developments and to cope with the resulting stress. In those cases individuals or groups are presented with a problem or situation and are required to find a solution either individually or by working in teams. In some cases an additional pressure is added by having individuals or groups compete to find the best solution in the shortest time. Problems can involve investment decisions, financial losses, manufacturing interruptions, employee relations, or even the development of an overall management plan for an organization or segment of an organization.

PROGRAM DEVELOPMENT

Regardless of the size or formality of a training need, it is important to develop programs in an organized and logical manner that will get the most value from the time and money invested. That means defining the goals and scope of each program, assessing the available resources, designing a thoughtful protocol, and scheduling sessions to maximize the learning process.

Goal Setting

Each training program should have a distinct and well-defined goal that can be used as a guide in structuring the program and against which the effectiveness of the training effort can be measured. The goal should include both the purpose and parameters of the program in specific terms. Formulating and stating the training goal is just as important in the less-formalized program as it is in a companywide training effort affecting a substantial number of employees.

When a single new employee is to be trained for a job in the small organization, the stated goal may be simply to teach the individual the procedures and methods outlined in the job description so that he can function independently within three weeks. As the program increases in complexity, the statement of purpose will change. Thus the goal for a full-scale management development program might be to increase the managerial skills of participants by providing an overview of the management function and personnel policies of the organization and equipping the participants with better planning, financial management, and employee relations skills. In each case, the routine and scope of the task have been delineated and, in fact, outlined. Once the broad goal has been stated, similar objectives may be set for each study unit as shown below.

Assessing Resources

Once the training needs and goals have been defined, it is necessary to assess the best means of achieving the desired results. There are a number of alternatives. The choice should be based on an expense/benefit basis. Will the expenses involved be justified by the potential benefit? How likely is the benefit to be achieved through the means under consideration?

IN-HOUSE PROGRAMS. The most frequently utilized programs are conducted by in-house trainers. In the case of the very small organization or department in which the greatest need is to train clerical or support personnel to handle routine assignments, the immediate supervisor or office (administrative) manager generally acts as trainer. In other cases the training function may be assigned to a specialist who develops and conducts training programs or acts as a resource to help supervisors develop programs to be repeated within the work unit. In assessing whether in-house resources ought to be utilized, three considerations should be addressed: the quality of in-house talent, the time expenditure involved, and the frequency of training needs.

The individuals assigned to the task must be capable of supplying the level of training required by the situation: interpersonal skills, ability to communicate, capability of developing and/or conducting the program, and knowledge of the subject. Individuals who might be excellent in a one-on-one training situation may not be able to lead a seminar or deliver a lecture; a supervisor may be able to conduct but not design a program; or an individual may be too new in his own position to be able to train others effectively.

In addition, it may be more costly in the long run to take supervisors away from production activities to train. It may be cheaper and more profitable to hire a specialist or seek outside training sources. Part of the decision will be based on the amount of training time required. In the larger organization in which a certain amount of turnover can be projected, especially in problem occupations, the amount of trainer time to be expended may be an indication of the need for specialist or outside help. Likewise, if the nature of the training requires the expenditure of protracted amounts of time, it may not be feasible to utilize line supervisors. For instance, when the technical skill to be taught must be followed by close and constant observation until the trainee has mastered the skill, supervisory resources may be inadequate to meet the objective.

CONSULTANTS. One outside resource is the consulting profession. Consultants can be obtained to develop and conduct a specialized course, such as a full-scale management course, on a long-term basis, or they can be hired to conduct seminars on predetermined topics, provide short-term training, or fill a void resulting from unusual in-house circumstances like the illness of a trainer, production emergencies, new supervisory staff, or a start-up situation. It is also possible to engage a consultant to design a training program geared to specific needs to be conducted by the supervisory staff on an ongoing basis. Such an arrangement may be effective when supervisors do not have the time or ability to design a program but will be able to implement a prestructured program.

STOCK PROGRAMS. Publishers and trade associations frequently have stock, or "canned," training programs available for sale or rent; such programs usually incorporate filmed lectures and demonstrations or cassette recordings. Although such programs can be well designed and executed, they have two drawbacks. They are designed for general consumption rather than for the particular organization. Unless they are conducted or supplemented by in-house personnel, they cannot offer the same personal training, "laboratory practice," or opportunity for individual questions and supplementary information. Therefore, it is better to use them as part of a personally conducted training course in which an instructor is available to provide additional input.

COMMUNITY RESOURCES. Not all training programs must be conducted within the organizational structure. It is often possible to arrange for educational courses for individuals or groups. Tuition assistance benefits and scholarships can provide additional education for employees on their own time or as part of a shared-time or work release program in which the time spent in class is partially or fully included in the normal workday. Some local boards of education or community colleges are willing to provide instructors to teach on company premises for a nominal sum. General education courses, business classes, or foreign language lessons can be conducted in that manner.

Sending top personnel to special seminars or short-term courses is another alternative. Educational institutions, trade associations, consultants, and professional organizations like the American Management Associations sponsor one-, two-, or three-day seminars on specialized topics. These can be most beneficial in sharpening needed skills and providing for the personal development of selected employees. High-level management courses of six or eight weeks frequently are part of the summer curricula of major universities.

Developing a Protocol

In designing a training course, attention must be given to four areas: the establishment of study units, selection of teaching techniques, the use of teaching aids, and the development of adequate testing mechanisms.

UNITS OF STUDY. A precise outline is needed to delineate each topic to be addressed, to work out a logical sequence of presenting the material, and, finally, to allocate a reasonable amount of time and emphasis. Each topic should be divided into study units which are subdivided to include each facet of the subject. Thus a protocol to train a new benefit clerk would include life insurance as a study unit and might be outlined as follows:

I. Types
   A. Contributory
      1. Amounts
      2. Eligibility
      3. Waiting period
      4. Cost
      5. Premium calculation
   B. Noncontributory
      1. Amounts
      2. Eligibility
      3. Waiting period
      4. Cost
      5. Premium calculation
II. Administration
   A. Enrollment procedures
      1. Enrollment cards
      2. Beneficiary designations
      3. Payroll forms
      4. Certificates and plan booklets
      5. Refusal of benefits
   B. Changes
      1. Beneficiary changes
      2. Name changes

3. Employee status changes
4. Termination of benefits
   a. Voluntary
   b. Termination of employment
5. Payroll forms

The outline would be continued to include billing and claims procedures for life insurance. Similar outlines or protocols would be developed for other forms of insurance to be processed by the employee. A similar plan should be devised for all training efforts including full-scale educational efforts. For instance, a managerial skills course could be divided into major topics such as work planning, career counseling, or goal setting. Each such topic should be outlined to insure the logical flow and inclusion of information. In a multiple-trainee course time estimates may be helpful to provide the trainer with a guideline for emphasis. Naturally, some flexibility is necessary in using lecture or discussion time, but it is essential to control the use of that time and to guard against time erosion by irrelevant or disproportionate amounts of discussion.

TECHNIQUES. The mode of training—individualized, lecture, seminar, or work simulation—must reflect both the nature of the material to be covered and the audience. Whatever the methodology, there are certain principles which should be observed in presenting the material.

First it is necessary to provide an overview of the topics, in-depth training, and a summary of information—the old-fashioned "tell them what you are going to do, do it, and tell them what you have done." Second, during the in-depth presentation, trainees must be given a frame of reference as well as procedural information; they must be taught what, how, where, who, and why. Finally, effective training requires both demonstration and participation. In addition to providing information, the trainer should provide an opportunity for trainee involvement either by active discussion or in practice time.

If someone outside the department conducts the training courses, care should be taken to coordinate training protocols with him. Trainee work schedules should be arranged to complement the course material both to provide reinforcement for study units and to take advantage of the trainees' developing skills. If possible, the supervisor should be included in the training sessions in some capacity.

TEACHING AIDS. The use of teaching aids to illustrate and reinforce the material covered in the course is invaluable. Graphic aids such as charts, blackboards, films, and slide presentations can be used to vary the pace, emphasize key points, or provide a focal point to a discussion. The aids need not be elaborate. Photocopies of graphs, statistical information, examples, or problems are simple and inexpensive to prepare. Lantern slides, also inexpensive and easily prepared, can be used as discussion outlines or to highlight key concepts. Films can be purchased or rented at reasonable cost to vary the pace, demonstrate the course material, and provide appropriate accent.

In formalized training programs and the less formal supervisor-trainee situations, the occupational manual is a very useful tool. It is simply a written explanation of each facet of the job on a topical or step-by-step basis. Examples of all forms, formats, calculation methods, formulas, lists of deadlines, and mailing and distribution lists and any other pertinent information should be included.

An occupational manual can provide an experienced individual in a new job situation with a handy guide to systems, departmental responsibilities, procedures, and formats peculiar to the organization. For the individual who requires more extensive training because he lacks experience or because of a unique job situation, it provides an invaluable reference guide. The trainer can use the manual to structure a protocol, and the supervisor is saved many interruptions by the existence of a written reference. Other employees or temporary help used to cope with extra work or substitute for sick or vacationing workers also will find an occupational guide useful.

Care must be taken not to substitute a manual for personal training. Neither should a manual be an excuse for a trainer to gloss over study material in a perfunctory manner. A manual should be used solely as a tool and reference text to supplement and structure training.

SCHEDULING. The scheduling of study units is important from three aspects: the absorption level of trainees, the interface between training and work sessions, and the continuity of production.

Trainee absorption levels should be reflected in the length of sessions and the amount and complexity of material to be covered in each study unit. Thus the material incorporated in each unit and the length of time allotted to the material must be geared to both topic and audience. Covering too much material in a session, especially if the topic is complex or technical, will erode the effectiveness of the training. It may be better to have more and shorter sessions to compensate for such material or for the learning capacity of the trainees. Care must be taken to allow for a difference in learning rates among individuals in a group situation.

Although it is inevitable that trainees will forget a portion of the material covered in any training course, such losses can be minimized by judicious interspersing of training and work sessions to allow people to practice newly learned skills. Whenever possible, each study topic should be scheduled to parallel production needs so that trainees will be exposed to the work situation after the training session. In the case of the benefit clerk discussed earlier, for instance, training may start with the billing process if a new employee begins work at the time a bill is due or with the claims process if the work flow so demands.

Even though production depends on adequate training, it is a rare situation that allows employees to be fully trained without simultaneous involvement in the production process. Therefore, it is usually necessary to schedule training sessions at a time of day when production will be least affected by worker attendance at training sessions or the use of work areas for training. The length and frequency of sessions also should reflect production demands.

FOLLOW-UP

Since training programs exist to fill a production need of one kind or another, it is only logical to emphasize the need to assure that training programs in fact are accomplishing their stated purpose. Hence the effect of training on production rates and personnel activity should be examined within the scope of the program's stated goal.

In some cases, the effect on production rates will be easy to determine by an increase in the quantity of goods or services

Figure 18. Training evaluation questionnaire.

Employee Name (optional) _____ Date _____

Job Title_____ Department _____ Start Date_____

Course Taken _____ Course Dates_____

1. Do you feel the course has helped you to do your job better?

    Yes ☐   No ☐

2. If yes, how?_____

_____

3. How would you rate the course in general?

    Poor ☐ Fair ☐ Acceptable ☐ Good ☐ Excellent ☐

4. What did you like best about the course?_____

_____

5. What did you like least? _____

_____

6. Did you think the instructor knew the subject? Yes ☐ No ☐

7. Was the subject presented in an interesting way? Yes ☐ No ☐

8. Were teaching aids — charts, slides, movies, etc. — used?   Yes ☐ No ☐

9. Did they help you learn?   Yes ☐ No ☐

10. How could the course be made better? _____

_____

_____

_____

_____

produced, reduction of backlog, or quality inspection reports. In other instances, results may not be measurable in statistically objective terms. Follow-up may require surveys of supervisors, department heads, or even clients. Employees also may be asked to fill out questionnaires (Figure 18) concerning their impressions of their own and their co-workers' development or skill acquisition as a result of the training effort.

With respect to individual employees, the most precise way to measure results is to test trainees at the end of the program. Follow-up tests after three or six months are effective in measuring long-term results and in determining whether reinforcement is needed or subsequent programs should be modified to increase their effectiveness. Other indications can be found in pre- and post-training performance reviews, grievances activity, and turnover statistics.

The results of such follow-up will determine whether training was effective, whether the increased production justified the expense, and how training programs can be improved—all practical and valuable statistics. However, results can be measured effectively only if the groundwork has been done prospectively; that is, the need has been documented and measurable goals have been established.

9 LEGISLATION

The employment milieu has been altered radically by the passage of a number of laws that regulate in great detail the entire scope of the ongoing process of employing people. The situation is made more difficult for employers by the continuous developments that have resulted from enforcement guidelines and court decisions and by the frequent amendments that often stem from changing economic conditions. Nonetheless, it is important to be familiar with the scope of existing legislation * and with the resources available for compliance and information update.

For organization purposes, employment-related legislation can be broken down into four categories: wage and salary, employment practices, safety, and benefits. Labor legislation will be discussed separately in Chapter 10.

WAGE-AND-SALARY ADMINISTRATION

The Fair Labor Standards Act of 1938 (FLSA) is a comprehensive law designed to eliminate "conditions detrimental to the maintenance of the minimum standard of living necessary for the health, efficiency, and general well-being of workers" in keeping with congressional power to protect and regulate commerce.† Amended several times to extend coverage and update wage provisions, this law regulates minimum wage and overtime compensation, equal pay, and child labor.

* This chapter is intended as a broad discussion of employment legislation, much of which is complex. Specific questions and problems require full knowledge of the circumstances and should be referred to legal counsel, a qualified consultant, or a technical expert from the enforcing agency.

† Fair Labor Standards Act of 1938 as amended, Section 2a and b.

Minimum Wages and Overtime

The FLSA provides that overtime be paid to covered workers, regulates overtime payment, and establishes record-keeping standards. It does not require time-off benefits for holidays, vacation, sick time and the like, provide for premium rates, or establish a limitation on hours worked.

COVERAGE. FLSA covers all employees directly or indirectly involved in interstate commerce and those who have some effect on interstate commerce. Thus, with rare exception, every regularly employed person, including domestic and agricultural employees, is covered under the Act without reference to the number of people employed by the organization. Not only workers paid salaries or hourly wages but also employees paid on the basis of commission, piecework, job rates, and the like are covered.

MINIMUM WAGE. The 1977 Amendment to FLSA provides that, effective January 1, 1978, the minimum wage be set at $2.65 per hour with specified exceptions. There are also provisions that the minimum wage be advanced to $2.90 on January 1, 1979, to $3.10 on January 1, 1980, and to $3.35 on January 1, 1981. Exemptions from the minimum wage can be obtained for full-time students, for whom certificates must be obtained in advance from the Secretary of Labor; such individuals must be paid 85 percent of the minimum wage. Similar provisions exist for handicapped workers.

OVERTIME COMPENSATION. Unless exempt from overtime provisions, employees must be paid one and one-half times their regular rate for all hours worked over 40 in any workweek. Overtime must be calculated on the basis of a fixed and permanent workweek (see Chapter 5). For employees paid on the basis of piecework, commission, bonuses, fluctuating hours, and similar variables, rates must be converted into hourly rates. *Overtime payment may not be waived.*

SPECIAL PROVISIONS. Because of special circumstances, certain occupations and industries are permitted to calculate overtime payments on a different basis. Public agencies may pay fire protection and law enforcement officers by utilizing 7- to 28-day work periods. Hospitals and residential care facilities may elect a 14-day work period; if they do so, they must pay the overtime rate for all hours worked over 8 in one day or over 80 in a work period. Previous exemptions for certain occupations that had been paid overtime for time worked over 48 hours were phased out by 1974 amendments.

EXEMPTIONS. FLSA exempts certain occupations from overtime payment, notably executives, administrative employees, professionals, and outside salesmen. However, there are very specific criteria for those exemptions. In broad terms, executives, administrative personnel, and professionals are defined as those to whom *all* of the following criteria apply.*

1. They have primary responsibility for managing an enterprise or customarily recognized department, perform nonmanual work involving management policy on general business operations, or perform original and creative work requiring advanced knowledge.
2. They direct the work of at least two other employees, including hiring and firing or participating in such decisions, or, under general supervision, assist a proprietor or executive by performing special assignments and tasks.
3. They must exercise independent and discretionary judgment.
4. They do not spend more than 20 percent of their hours (40 percent in retail and service establishments) in nonexempt work.
5. They receive a specified minimum salary.

TIME WORKED. "Time worked" includes all the time an employee works or is permitted to work. That is, it includes any time he is required to be at his work station or is waiting to be assigned work, as well as interruptions during meal breaks, training time, and the like. If an employee voluntarily works beyond his assigned shift or at home, he must be paid. It is up to the employer to enforce overtime authorization policies and to control the working time of all personnel.

* *Defining the Terms "Executive," "Administrative," "Professional," and "Outside Salesman,"* U.S. Department of Labor, Employment Standards Administration, Wage and Hour Division, WH Publication 1281 (revised 1975), Sections 541.1–541.3.

RECORD KEEPING. The burden is on the employer to provide acceptable documentation of time worked. Record keeping is discussed in detail in Chapter 5.

PAYMENT. In general, overtime should be paid on the regular payday for the pay period in which the work was performed. If the correct amount of overtime cannot be calculated in time for the regular pay day, it should be paid as soon as possible.

Child Labor

In general, the minimum age for employment is 16. There are two exceptions: a minimum age of 18 for occupations defined as hazardous, and an exception for 14- and 15-year-olds in certain jobs when the hours do not conflict with school schedules. "Oppressive" child labor practices are prohibited, and there are special provisions regarding children employed in agriculture.

Equal Pay Act

The Equal Pay Amendment of 1974 prohibits pay discrimination because of sex. It provides that men and women working in the same establishment under similar conditions must be paid equally if their jobs require equal skill, effort, and responsibility and if working conditions are similar. That means equal experience, training, education, and physical or mental exertion. Intermittent extra physical exertion or a minor or insignificant difference in the degree of responsibility does not make the *jobs* unequal. Differentials paid on the basis of head-of-household status, traditional male advancement potential, training, costs, titles, and such are unlawful. The only valid reasons for pay differences are those directly related to job requirements, performance, seniority, or production-related systems. Premiums for undesirable shifts are permitted so long as the practice does not result in discrimination, as when only men are hired for such shifts.

Court rulings concerning the Equal Pay Amendment have emphasized the use of objective criteria for establishing wage differentials between jobs and have focused on the need to establish job evaluation systems in which each job is rated individually (see Chapter 3). However, the courts have also considered the effects of employment practices on pay practices. Hence, even if pay differentials can be justified by job title or shift assignment, discrimination has been found to exist if only men are hired to fill certain vacancies.

ENFORCEMENT. The Secretary of Labor is empowered to enforce the Act. He and his designated representative have specific authority to establish regulations and standards, investigate wage and payment practices, inspect records, and require reports regarding any provisions of the Act. Moreover, the Secretary is authorized to supervise payment of any wages due employees under the Act or bring suit against any employer for collection of monies due employees under the law. The Wage and Hour Division of the Department of Labor is the administering agency.

Wage Garnishment

The Federal Wage Garnishment Law limits the amount of an employee's disposable earnings which may be garnished and defines the legal restrictions and employee's rights connected with garnishments. It does not negate the rights of the creditor to collect the full amount owned to him, but it limits the amount that can be deducted from the employee's pay check.

GARNISHMENT DEFINED. Garnishment means any legal or equitable procedure requiring that an employee's wages be withheld for payment of a debt. By definition, therefore, there must be a court judgment before deductions from pay checks can be made. In addition, even wage assignments are permissible only after court proceedings.

RESTRICTIONS. The Law imposes restrictions on what portion of the employee's wages are subject to garnishment and how much may be deducted for such a purpose. To begin with, the Law defines as "disposable earnings" that part of an employee's earnings left after legally required deductions have been made, particularly, federal, state, and city taxes and state-required retirement deductions. That excludes voluntary deductions for such items as savings bonds, charitable contributions, and union dues. In addition, it limits the amount of deductions that can be made each pay period. A maximum of 25 percent of the employee's disposable earnings can be deducted provided that disposable earnings exceed 30 times the federal minimum wage $(30 \times \$2.90 = \$87)$. Thus, only 25 percent of "disposable" income above $87 per week, or $21.75, can be deducted for wage garnishment purposes. For employees paid on other than a weekly basis, wages must be treated as a unit; for example, earnings of $60 the first week of a two-week pay period and $140 in the second equal $100 weekly earnings.

PROTECTION FROM DISCHARGE. The Law prohibits the discharge of an employee because his wages have been garnished for *any one indebtedness*. Thus if wages are garnished more than once for the same debt, an employee cannot be terminated; if wages are garnished for additional debts, an employee may be discharged under the terms of this law. However, the Equal Employment Opportunity Commission has found that, since certain minority groups are more likely to have multiple wage garnishments, discharge for such cause may be discriminatory. Therefore, any policy relating to discharge for multiple garnishments should conform to EEOC guidelines as well.

EMPLOYMENT PRACTICES

Legislation regulating employment practices began with the passage of the Civil Rights Acts of 1866 and 1870, which prohibited private, public, and state acts of discrimination on the basis of color. Over the years various executive orders were issued to prohibit discrimination and promote equal opportunity. At this time there are five major laws to be considered. The most far-reaching is Title VII of the Civil Rights Act of 1964 as amended in 1972 and as supplemented by various executive orders, governmental guidelines, and court decisions. Others include the Equal Pay Act of 1963, which was discussed earlier in this chapter, the Age Discrimination Act of 1967, the Fair Credit Reporting Act, which took effect in 1971, the Vocational Rehabilitation Act of 1973, and the Vietnam Era Veterans' Readjustment Act of 1974.

The Civil Rights Act

Title VII of the 1964 Civil Rights Act as amended by the Equal Employment Opportunity Act of 1972 is the basis for sweeping reforms in employment practices. Designed to enforce the constitutional rights of individuals, this law has created an aggressive enforcing agency and has triggered extensive legal proceedings and court rulings.

THE LAW. The main thrust of Title VII is the declaration that it is unlawful "to fail or refuse to hire or to discharge" an individual or to discriminate "with respect to his compensation, terms, conditions, or privileges of employment" on the basis of race, color, religion, sex, or national origin *or* to "limit, segregate, or classify employees or applicants in any way that would deprive or tend to deprive any individual of employment opportunities or otherwise adversely affect his status as an employee" because of race, color, religion, sex, or national origin.* Similar prohibitions are placed on employment agencies in referring applicants and on labor unions in membership criteria and referral policies.

COVERAGE. Employers of 15 or more employees, for 20 or more calendar weeks, are subject to the provisions of Title VII if they are engaged in an industry, business, or activity affecting interstate commerce. In addition, special provisions are made for contractors, public employers, and the like. In short, with rare exceptions, every employer of more than 14 people is subject to the law even if employees work in different locations.

RECRUITMENT AND SELECTION. Guidelines concerning the recruitment and selection of new employees can be broken down into five categories.

1. Advertising and job notices. Recruiting must be conducted in a nonrestrictive manner. Classified advertisements should carry no references to race, color, religion, sex, national origin, or age. Hence, no ads should be placed in Help Wanted—Male or Help Wanted—Female columns. Such terms as "young," "boy," "girl," "recent college graduate," and "retired person" should be eliminated. Advertising invalid requirements or preferences such as educational levels is considered unlawful. Word-of-mouth recruiting or reliance on employee referrals is prohibited if minorities are likely to be underrepresented in the resulting labor pool. Advertisements should include a statement identifying the employer as an Equal Opportunity Employer, M-F. Employment agencies should be notified in writing of equal opportunity policies and requested to make referrals without discrimination.

2. Prehire inquiries. This term refers to any information re-

---

* The Equal Employment Opportunity Act of 1972, Section 703(a).

quested verbally or in writing, including questions asked by an interviewer and requested on résumé forms. No minority, female, or older applicant should be asked for any information not required of all applicants. That includes questions regarding children, child care, family planning, health, and sources of income. Questions regarding citizenship, place of birth, arrest records, and military discharges may be construed as discriminatory.

These prohibitions do not apply when there are bona fide and nondiscriminatory justifications such as insuring that an alien is eligible to work under immigration laws or seeking information regarding criminal *convictions* if the employee will have access to the personal property of clients. However, such exceptions must be valid and not a subterfuge for discrimination.

It is a recommended practice to include on application forms a brief statement of the intent of the Civil Rights and Age Discrimination Acts and company policy not to discriminate.

3. Testing. The use of test results as a basis for employment decisions is fraught with pitfalls. "Test" is defined as "all formal, scored, quantified or standardized techniques of assessing job qualifications" including "paper and pencil" tests, performance measurements, scored interviews and forms, rating scales, and the like. Although modified EEOC guidelines have eliminated the need to validate all tests before their inclusion in the selection process, employers are required to validate tests if the selection rate for any minority group is less than 80 percent of the rate for the group with the highest rating. Such a requirement implies a need to monitor testing programs. The burden is on the employer to insure that testing programs do not discriminate, even unintentionally.

4. Selection criteria. Employers may fail or refuse to hire any applicant for valid reasons such as lack of ability or experience or failure to meet physical requirements. However, the decision must be based on bona fide job requirements. To base employment decisions on criteria such as client or co-worker preference, company image, superior or inferior abilities relating to nonessential factors, length of training period, tradition, domestic responsibilities, stereotypes, job classifications, and invalid height-weight requirements is clearly prohibited. In short, only bona fide job requirements and the individual's ability should be

criteria. Although the law does not require that minorities and females be given preferential consideration, such a policy would not be considered discriminatory.

5. Rejection rates. When the rejection rate for one group is higher than that for another, the employer may be required to validate employment standards. Selection criteria must accurately predict ability to perform the essential duties of the job and/or relate to other performance "domains" including critical or important work behaviors and job duties.*

CONDITIONS OF EMPLOYMENT. Civil rights legislation also requires that employees be treated without discrimination with respect to the "terms, conditions, and privileges of employment." Thus, the employer must provide an unbiased working environment and is responsible for his own actions and those of all employees. Several policy areas deserve special consideration:

1. Assignments. Employees must be assigned work, hours, and breaks without discrimination. That is, it is illegal to refuse overtime, night shifts, job classifications, titles, and work groups on the basis of race, color, religion, sex, or national origin. When, for instance, employees request a schedule that would allow them time for the observance of a religious practice, a reasonable effort must be made to accommodate them. Likewise, a woman cannot be refused overtime or night shifts "for her own protection."

2. Promotion, transfer, seniority. Whatever system of promotions or transfer is used must be nondiscriminatory in effect as well as intent. A line of progression may be invalid, for instance, if jobs involving physical strength are placed in the line of progression to ban the advancement of females; a seniority system might be suspect if certain groups lack seniority because of past discrimination; and personal evaluations must be nondiscriminatory.

3. Dress codes. Grooming standards must be reasonable and appropriate. The existence of dress codes for one sex and not the other, different rules for hair length, and similar restrictions may be discriminatory. Prohibition of dress and grooming practices related to ethnic or religious backgrounds is discriminatory.

---

* "Guideline on Employee Selection Procedures," Prentice-Hall Personnel Management, Englewood Cliffs, N.J.: Prentice-Hall, Inc., 11, 940-B-C.

4. Use of facilities. In-house facilities such as lunchrooms, cafeterias, recreational areas, social clubs, and housing must be available on a nondiscriminatory basis. Refusal to hire or assign individuals of one sex because rest room facilities are not available is prohibited; appropriate facilities must be provided for both sexes.

5. Leave benefits. In granting time off, an employer must make a reasonable effort to accommodate the religious needs of his employees. Males and females of the same status must receive equal holiday pay, sick leave, and vacation time. An extended leave without pay for maternity should be treated as any other leave without pay. Requiring a pregnant employee to cease work and limiting her return to specified times is unlawful. Such decisions should be made on an individual basis depending on the woman's decision and her ability or inability to perform her job. Since the maternity leave issue is the subject of ongoing court decisions and controversy, it is wise to keep abreast of all developments.

6. Benefits. Employee benefit programs must be nondiscriminatory; equal benefits must be provided for both sexes. If insurance coverage is available for wives and children of male employees, it must be provided for the husbands and children of females. A clause specifying dependent status is lawful. Insurance coverage may not limit maternity benefits to married women. Eligibility for insurance and disability programs may not be based on head-of-household status.*

DISCHARGE. Involuntary termination of an employee must be based on the individual's inability to perform his job or on consistent and nondiscriminatory policies governing excessive absenteeism, failure to observe established rules, and similar performance standards. However, care must be taken that such discharges do not result in unintentional discrimination. For instance, discharge for garnishment for multiple debts may result in discrimination if certain social minorities are found to be affected in disproportionate numbers. Objective documentation of all involuntary discharges and the events leading to them is essential.

AFFIRMATIVE ACTION. Equal opportunity guidelines stress that,

---

* "Guidelines on Discrimination Because of Sex," Title 29, Labor, Chapter XIV, Part 1604, as amended March 1972.

in addition to avoiding deliberate discrimination, employers should take positive action to see that current employment practices are nondiscriminatory and to correct the effects of past discrimination by taking "affirmative action." An affirmative-action plan is a statement of an employer's program to achieve equal opportunity. It should detail specific goals, usually based on labor pool population, for the employment and promotion of minorities and women, a table and explanation of job classifications, descriptions, and rate of pay, and an analysis of the utilization of females and minorities. There should be a breakdown of minority and female representation of each job category, as well as hiring practices and promotions for the preceding year.

Although all employers are encouraged to adopt such plans, affirmative action is *required* of all contractors and subcontractors of the federal government when the contract involves $50,000 or more (or $500,000 for construction contractors or subcontractors of federal or federally assisted construction projects).*

ENFORCEMENT. Title VII created an Equal Employment Opportunity Commission to administer and enforce the provisions of the Civil Rights Act. The Commission, headed by five commissioners appointed by the President, is empowered to set guidelines for compliance, require reports from employers subject to Title VII, investigate charges of discrimination, and file a civil action on behalf of a plaintiff.

In addition to the Commission's Washington, D.C., headquarters, there are seven regional offices and 32 district offices to administer guidelines to serve as a liaison with local government and private agencies. The basic system for processing a charge of discrimination begins with the filing of the charge by an individual or his representative(s) or by one of the commissioners. The EEOC then investigates practices of the charged party. If probable cause is determined, there is an attempt to conciliate so that unfair practices can be eliminated voluntarily. If conciliation fails, EEOC may file suit to achieve court-ordered compliance. Often the initial contact with the employer will be made by a state or local agency to whom EEOC defers for 60 to 120 days.

* "Public Contracts and Property Management," Title 41, Chapter 60, Section 60–1.40, and Executive Orders No. 11246 and 11375.

Investigatory procedures are extensive and are not limited to the particular action that prompted the charge. Typically, a review is made of all similar transactions for six months prior to the alleged discriminatory act. (See record-keeping requirements as discessed in Chapter 5.) If no probable violation of the law is found, EEOC will withdraw and notify the plaintiff of his right to file a civil action. The plaintiff also has a right to sue if the Commission does not act within 180 days of the official filing date. If there is probable violation, persuasion and conciliation are pursued before legal action is taken. Voluntary correction may involve only the plaintiff or may involve a class of applicants or employees. Usually settlements are retroactive to the date of violation.

REPORTS. Employers of 100 or more individuals are required to file annual reports (EEOC-1) with the Equal Employment Opportunity Commission. The report is designed to allow analysis of minority and female employment within the various job categories: officials and managers, professionals, technical, office and clerical, and service workers. It also shows the racial distribution—Caucasians, Negroes, American Indians, Orientals, and Spanish surnames—of males and females within those categories. Note that, in gathering data for such reports, it is recommended that the information be obtained visually and that no direct inquiries be made.

Age Discrimination in Employment Act of 1967

The Age Discrimination Act covers employers of 20 or more employees and prohibits discrimination against individuals between 40 and 60 years old. It is unlawful for employers to fail or refuse to hire or to discharge or otherwise discriminate on the basis of age in matters of compensation or other employment-related matters.

The guidelines for compliance with age discrimination legislation are close to those in force for Title VII with respect to recruiting practices and advertising (although no affirmative-action statements are required for age), work assignment, discipline, benefits, and discharge. An employer cannot refuse to hire an individual receiving old-age social security benefits, for instance, but he is not required to adjust a work schedule to accommodate wage-earning restrictions. A compensation differ-

202 | PERSONNEL MANAGEMENT FOR THE SMALLER COMPANY

entiation may be justified by a bona fide benefit plan, but no such plan can be used as a reason not to hire.

The Act is administered by the Secretary of Labor through the Employment Standards Administration the Wage and Hour Division. Enforcement provisions are similar to those of the Fair Labor Standards Act; the Secretary is empowered to seek voluntary compliance, seek legal action, and supervise the collections of monies due individuals because of discriminatory acts.

Fair Credit Reporting Act

The Fair Credit Reporting Act regulates credit bureau reporting by defining the permissible uses and levels of consumer reports, by establishing guidelines for investigations, and by requiring that certain information be provided to "consumers," in this case the employee or applicant. The intent of the law is to protect the individual by requiring reasonable reporting procedures and proper utilization of information. (Note, however, that this law pertains only to the use of outside credit-reporting agencies and does not apply to an employer whose personnel check references or verify any information revealed on the application or in an interview.)

The law distinguishes between a consumer report that supplies information on credit, character, general reputation, and similar material to be used in evaluating an individual for employment, promotion, reassignment, or retention and an investigative report that provides similar information. The difference lies in the means of collecting information; the investigative report is based on personal interviews with neighbors, friends, associates, and acquaintances.

Consumer reports can be used for employment purposes. For positions involving an annual salary of less than $20,000 a year, the law prohibits inclusion of obsolete material, that is, adverse information regarding bad debts, arrest, indictment or conviction records, and the like antedating the report by seven years.

When investigative consumer reports are used in connection with employment opportunities for which a person has applied, the employer must advise the applicant or employee in writing within three days that such a report may be made. The individual must be notified in writing that, within a reasonable length of time, he has the right to request in writing complete disclosure on the nature and scope of the report requested. If he makes such a request, the employer must provide the information in writing within five days. The credit reporting agency, upon written request by the individual, must supply information from its files. The employer has no obligations in this area; he must advise the credit agency prospectively of his identification and certifications as to the purpose and restricted use of the report.

Whichever type of report is used, when employment is denied *on the basis* of a consumer report, the employer is required to advise the individual of that fact in writing and supply the name and address of the agency that furnished the information.

The implications involved in the law make it impractical in most cases to use consumer reporting agencies unless positions have great significance within the organization or involve particular security considerations.

Although no restrictions are placed on the employer whose personnel check references, it is advisable to include on the application form a statement, to be signed by the applicant, authorizing a reference check, stipulating the probationary employment period, and acknowledging that false statements are grounds for dismissal. In some states, a release of that kind may be mandatory.

Vocational Rehabilitation Act of 1973

The Vocational Rehabilitation Act of 1973 prohibits employers holding a federal contract for $2,500 or more from discriminating against, and requires them to take affirmative action to hire, qualified handicapped persons. "Handicap" is defined as a physical or mental impairment, record, or appearance of such impairment that substantially limits one or more of the applicant's life functions—including his employability, communication, ambulation, self-care, and transportation. People who are blind, paraplegic, have histories of mental illness, cancer, heart conditions, mental retardation, or the appearance of mental retardation are examples of those covered under this law. Individuals must be qualified in terms of job specifications and reasonable accommodation to their handicaps.

Employers with government contracts for $50,000 or more who have at least 50 employees must develop and maintain a formal affirmative-action plan including a review of job requirements, reasonable accommodations to employee limitations, and outreach in recruiting efforts. Job applicants who want to be considered under affirmative-action programs may be asked to identify themselves to the contractor. Confidentiality must be maintained except for those with a need to know, including supervisors, managers, and health care personnel.

The Employment Standards Administration of the Department of Labor administers this law.

Vietnam Era Veterans' Readjustment Act of 1974

Employers with federal contracts of $10,000 or more are required by the Vietnam Era Veterans' Readjustment Act not to discriminate against qualified individuals because they are veterans of that era or because of their disabilities. Veterans of the era are those with active service for more than 180 days between August 5, 1964, and May 7, 1975, with other than dishonorable discharges or releases or with service-connected disabilities. Veterans must have been released within 48 months. Disabled veterans are those entitled to Veterans Administration disability compensation of 30 percent or more or those discharged or released from active duty because of a disability incurred in or aggravated by that service.

As with the handicapped, veterans must be qualified in terms of job specifications and, in the case of the disabled, to have made reasonable accommodation to the disability. Affirmative-action stipulations parallel those required under the above legislation.

This law is administered by the Office of Federal Contract Compliance of the Employment Standards Administration of the Department of Labor.

SAFETY

The Williams-Steiger Occupational Safety and Health Act of 1970 (OSHA) sets standards for the maintenance of safe and healthful working conditions. The law sets specific standards which must be observed, requires employers to keep records and file reports of work-related deaths, illnesses, injuries, and hazards, and provides for inspections. All employers engaged in a business affecting commerce are covered by the Act.

Standards

In general, employers are required to furnish "employment and places of employment free from recognized hazards causing, or likely to cause, death or serious physical harm." * Employers are required to comply with safety and health regulations established in accordance with the legislation.

Thousands of standards covering a broad spectrum of occupations have been developed. For the most part the standards are based on those adopted by the American Standards Institute and the National Fire Protection Association. Some are general, outlining housekeeping responsibilities, fire protection measures, life-safety codes, sanitary facilities, and so forth. Others are quite specific and regulate particular industries, processes, and equipment. For instance, there are standards for spray finishing using flammable and combustible materials, indoor general storage, pulp, paper, and paperboard industries, laundry machinery and operations, air contaminants, materials handling and storage, electrical appliances, safety equipment, and hosts of others. A complete list of standards is contained in the January 1976 *Federal Register*. In addition, the Department of Labor maintains National and Regional Offices for the Occupational Safety and Health Administration and its Office of Information Services.

RECORD KEEPING. OSHA requires that employers keep on a calendar basis, a day-to-day log of all work-related deaths, illnesses, and injuries requiring medical treatment, including dates, diagnoses, names, titles or job descriptions, amount of time lost, transfers or reassignments, and a description of treatment. (OSHA Form 100 has been developed for the purpose.) Supplementary records (OSHA Form 101, workmen's compensation records, or similar forms) must be kept for each recordable incident. The records, which must be maintained for five years, must include the following: name, address, and site of employer; name, address, age, sex, social security number, occupation, and department of employee; circumstances of the accident or injury; and any applicable treatment information. In addition, employers can be required to record employee expo-

* *Recordkeeping Requirements Under the Occupation Safety and Health Act of 1970*, U.S. Department of Labor, Occupational Safety and Health Administration, p. 4.

sure to potentially toxic materials or other agents and to advise employees of the exposure and corrective action.

ENFORCEMENT. The major enforcement authority lies with the Occupational Safety and Health Administration under the Secretary of Labor and an Occupational Safety and Health Review Commission appointed by the President. The Secretary of Health, Education and Welfare has additional functions to be carried out by the National Institute for Occupational Safety and Health. States are encouraged to assume enforcement and administrative responsibility.

Both the Labor Department and HEW have the right to inspect employer premises as the result of a complaint or as part of an administrative inspection schedule. An authorizing warrant is required. Employers and employee representatives are permitted to accompany inspectors. Employers may be required to conduct their own inspections. Violations can result in heavy financial penalties if not corrected in timely fashion.

BENEFITS

As discussed earlier in this chapter, the Civil Rights Act had a significant impact on benefits by requiring that all benefits be made available on a nondiscriminatory basis. But several other major areas are subject to regulation, specifically retirement plans, health care, workmen's compensation, and unemployment insurance.

Retirement Plans

The Welfare and Pension Plans Disclosure Act of 1958, which was amended in 1962, required that employers develop and file with the Department of Labor descriptions of pension plans, financial reports, and other pertinent information. The law was replaced by a more comprehensive piece of legislation, the Employee's Retirement Income Security Act of 1974 (ERISA), which addresses itself to all phases of retirement plan administration.

The main thrust of ERISA is to protect the rights of participants in employee benefit plans, and their beneficiaries, by insuring the equitability and soundness of retirement income plans. Thus the law encompasses all aspects of retirement plans from eligibility to funding and includes Internal Revenue Service regulations. This discussion is intended to provide a nontechnical overview with an emphasis on administrative rather than actuarial considerations.

COVERAGE. The term "retirement income plan" means any plan providing deferred income to participants. Hence, individual account plans, defined benefit plans, multiple- or single-employer plans, pensions, excess benefit plans, stock allocation plans, deferred profit-sharing plans, *any* retirement plan must be a written instrument conforming to ERISA standards if it is established and maintained by an employer and/or organization engaged in or representing employees engaged in commerce.

DISCLOSURE AND REPORTING. The plan's administrator must furnish participants and beneficiaries with a summary plan description and information about plan changes or modifications. The material must be designed to be understood by the average participant. Annual financial statements must be distributed, and plan summaries must be updated every five years. A comprehensive plan description, summary plan description, and *annual* financial statements and reports must be furnished to the Secretary of Labor, as must any modifications or changes, qualification data, financial status, and general operations. Participants and beneficiaries are entitled to request written statements regarding accrued and vested benefits.

ELIGIBILITY. The waiting period for inclusion can be no longer than one year's employment (1,000 working hours); the exception is a three-year waiting period if benefits are 100% vested after that time. It is lawful to require that an individual be 25 years old before being eligible for a plan with deferred vesting or 30 for a plan with immediate vesting. No plan except a defined-benefit plan may exclude employees who have reached any specified age; a defined-benefit plan is one in which the benefit is fixed and contributions are variable. That may exclude employees who begin employment within five years of normal retirement age.

PARTICIPATION. At least 70 percent of all employees or 80 percent of employees eligible to benefit under the plan must be covered for the plan to qualify under Internal Revenue Service codes. This excludes seasonal employees and those who do not meet the age and service requirements described above. It includes those who have passed the maximum age. This provision prohibits discrimination in favor of officers, highly compensated individuals, and other special interest groups.

VESTING. The employees' contributions must be 100 percent vested immediately. There are three alternative vesting requirements with respect to employer contributions. The first is a proscribed schedule under which vesting increases yearly from 25 percent at 5 years to 100 percent at 15 years. The second provides 100 percent vesting after 10 years of participation in the plan. The third alternative is a vesting schedule covering employees who have at least 5 years of participation and whose combined age and participation time equals 45 or more. Benefits of employees with 5 years of service whose age plus covered service equals or exceeds 45 must be 50 percent vested, and all employees with 10 years of service must receive 50 percent vesting with an additional 10 percent of vesting for each additional year of service.

BENEFIT LIMITATION. In defined-benefit programs the benefit is limited to the lower of $75,000 annually or .100 percent of the average compensation received in the individual's highest three years of employment compensation. In defined-contribution plans the annual contribution is limited to $25,000 or 25 percent of the employee's compensation for the year. No plan may discriminate in favor of highly compensated employees, officers, or other "elite" personnel.

BENEFIT ACCRUAL. The means by which benefits are accrued are regulated. In defined-contribution plans, the accrued amount is always the amount in the individual's "account." Accruals under defined-benefit plans are subject to specific formulas depending on the type of plan. Factors such as normal retirement age, length of participation, and normal retirement benefits are included in the calculation.

LOSS OR SUSPENSION OF BENEFITS. A plan may provide for the forfeiture of *employer* contributions if the employee dies before retirement. A retired employee who returns to work for his employer may have his benefits suspended for the duration of that employment. If an employee whose benefits are less than 50 percent vested with respect to employer contributions withdraws his mandatory contributions, the benefit attributed to employer contributions may be forfeited. A terminating employee with a benefit value of less than $1,750 may be given a lump sum payment.

FUNDING STANDARDS. Plans must establish and maintain "funding standard accounts" into which must be paid the normal costs for a plan year plus amounts necessary to amortize the plan plus reserves necessitated by deficiencies or experience. Experience gains and losses must be calculated regularly.

RECORD KEEPING. Separate individual accounts are required for employee contributions and defined-benefit plans. Records must be maintained to determine benefits that are or may become due or to furnish accrued benefit reports to participants, beneficiaries, terminating employees, and the like. Records pertaining to annual reports, including worksheets, vouchers, and receipts, must be available for examination for at least six years after the filing date.

PLAN TERMINATION. Special provisions regulate procedures to be followed when plans are involuntarily or voluntarily terminated. They include trustee appointments and management and/or allocation of assets. ERISA also established a nonprofit Pension Benefit Guarantee Corporation to insure participants and beneficiaries against loss of benefits.

ENFORCEMENT. Responsibility for the administration and enforcement of ERISA is split between the Department of Labor and the Treasury. The Internal Revenue Service has jurisdiction over the funding, participation, and vesting provisions of the law and is charged with determining the tax qualifications of the plan. The Labor Department is concerned with the administration of plans in terms of fiduciary responsibility, including record keeping and communications with participants and beneficiaries.

Health Care

The Health Maintenance Organization Act of 1973 requires that employers of 25 or more who are subject to the minimum wage provisions of the Fair Labor Standards Act of 1938 offer their employees the option of membership in a health maintenance organization if their location is served by a qualified HMO and if a qualified HMO approaches them with a proposal. Employers are not required to form or seek out an HMO.

HMO QUALIFICATIONS. To meet the standards of the law, the HMO must provide specified services to its members, including physician services, inpatient and outpatient hospital services, emergency health service, diagnostic and therapeutic radiological services, diagnostic laboratories, home and preventive dental and medical services, mental health facilities and supplemental services for intermediate and long-term care, vision care, long-term physical medicine and rehabilitation, and provision of prescription drugs. The organization, staffing, and operations of HMO's are subject to comprehensive proscriptions.

COSTS. The emphasis of the HMO is on the maintenance of good health and prevention of illness. The attainment of such goals would lead, logically, to a reduction in expenditures for treatment of illnesses. The periodic payment to the HMO could be likened to an insurance premium, which is a "prepayment" of the benefits that will eventually be claimed. Therefore, the law stipulates that no employer will be required to pay more to provide the HMO option to his employees than he normally would pay for health care benefits. Likewise, there is a provision limiting the cost to HMO enrollees to nominal copayments for supplemental health services.

Unemployment Insurance

Unemployment insurance is designed to cover those who are subject to the risks of "involuntary unemployment." Since unemployment insurance is regulated and administered on a state-by-state basis, the benefits and supportive taxes vary. However, federal legislation as administered by the Manpower Administration of the U.S. Department of Labor assures that all state plans meet certain requirements.

ELIGIBILITY. Each state must develop criteria for determining eligibility. Workers must have had recent employment of sufficient duration to qualify for benefits. Generally, there is a requirement that the individual has worked a minimum number of weeks in covered employment at a specified average minimum wage or that the worker earned wages in a "base period" within the calendar quarter.

AMOUNT OF BENEFITS. The amount of unemployment benefits will vary with earnings and location. Federal guidelines require that weekly benefits amount to at least one-half the usual weekly wage of the general population (not the individual claimant) and that the maximum benefit be high enough that 80 percent of the insured workers are assured of receiving 50 percent of their usual earnings. In some states the unemployed worker will receive a base benefit plus additional amounts for dependents.

DURATION. Since unemployment insurance is designed to provide the covered worker with income during *temporary* periods of unemployment, there is a limit to how long the worker will be eligible to receive benefits. Some states base payment periods on the amount of past earnings or employment; others have a uniform period, usually 26 weeks. In periods of high unemployment, the duration of benefits may be extended.

CONDITIONS. Unemployment insurance is designed to provide a resource for those who are *involuntarily* unemployed. Therefore, individuals are ineligible for benefits under certain conditions:

1. Voluntarily leaving work without good cause
2. Discharge for work-related misconduct
3. Refusing suitable work
4. Involvement in a labor dispute
5. Fraudulent application for benefits

Typically, such disqualifications are defined by the individual state; that is, "suitability" may be interpreted as the suitability of work for the individual and may vary with the opportunities in specific geographic or economic circumstances. Some states require that recipients register with the state employment service or appear in person to collect payments and report on job-seeking efforts.

FINANCING. Unemployment insurance is financed by an employer-paid tax based on payroll; both the percent of tax and the amount of payroll subject to tax vary from state to state. Additional payment may be required from employers with excessive claims. Tax rates are based on the amount of money needed to fund payments and to provide a reserve against high claims. Since the employer pays the costs regardless of the system, it is in his interest to avoid unjustified claims. The discipline and termination procedures discussed in Chapter 5 and maintenance of proper documentation are the key to cost-containment efforts. Proper record keeping also is necessary. For instance, discharge for cause should be stated in explicit terms rather than "sugar-coating" the transaction by calling it a lay-off or a "mutual agreement." No employee should be asked to resign. It is important to remember that an employee is discharged only because his actions warrant the termination.

CHALLENGING A CLAIM. When a former employee submits a claim for unemployment compensation, he must list his employers of record, dates of employment, and wages for a specified period, usually for the preceding and current calendar years. The employer is contacted by the state agency to verify the information. The last employer of record also has the opportunity to challenge the claim if the claimant should be disqualified. That may mean that the employer or a qualified representative must appear at a disqualification hearing at which both parties testify about the circumstances of the termination. Organizations with high turnover often contract with a firm to keep track of claims, control records, and represent them in hearings.

Workmen's Compensation

Like unemployment insurance, workmen's compensation is legislated and administered by the individual states. The purpose of the legislation is, of course, to provide equitable compensation and medical costs for the individual with a work-related illness, injury, or disability.

COVERAGE. For the most part workmen's compensation is provided through commercial insurance companies, but some states have their own insurance pool into which employers pay. In either case, payment usually is based on a fixed schedule of benefits depending on the nature of the work-related illness or injury.

COST CONTAINMENT. Whether commercial insurance or a state plan is involved, costs will rise with claims experience. There are several steps that can be taken to avoid unnecessary costs. First, it is important to hire people who are able to meet the physical requirements of the job. In some cases it may be advisable to get medical clearance before hiring an individual with a history of physical injuries or chronic ailments that have a bearing on the job. Employees should be trained in safety procedures and required to follow safety regulations, including the use of safety equipment. Some insurance companies publish claims reports for specific industries that provide insight into problem areas and suggest remedies. Employers with high claims may find it worthwhile to purchase insurance through an insurance broker or administrator who will provide backup inspections and claims control. Or, a safety consultant may be helpful. Since a high incidence of work-related injuries may be related to OSHA violations, safety standards should be studied with an eye to correcting problem areas. A safe physical plant is essential whether it involves stable bases for typewriters or proper guardrails for vats of acid.

STATE LEGISLATION

Each state has a host of laws which regulate different phases of employee relations. Information can be obtained either through the state labor department or commercial publishers. In some instances state legislation will supplement or parallel federal regulations; in other cases, state law will involve more detailed transactions. For example, one state requires that an employee being terminated for cause must receive his final pay check immediately, and another requires that such payment be made within five days of termination. In any case it is necessary to know the law.

Generally, state laws that are more restrictive stand unless they conflict with federal legislation. For instance, certain states have "protective" laws restricting the employment of women to certain hours or prohibiting women from lifting heavy weights, and so on. Since those laws are held to be in conflict with civil rights legislation and the constitutional rights of women, the federal law takes precedence.

COMPLIANCE

In general, failure to comply with the legislation described above can result in heavy financial penalties either in fines or back pay. In addition to requiring that the employer follow the dictates of such legislation, the laws specifically require that employees and/or applicants be advised that they are covered by the law. This means employers must exhibit in prominent areas any poster developed by the federal agencies to describe coverage. It also means that it is illegal for any employer to discharge, harass, or otherwise retaliate against any employee who claims his rights under any law, makes charges or requests inspections by the enforcing agencies, or advises another individual of his rights.

10 LABOR UNIONS

Few issues tend to be as disruptive to management as the introduction of a union into the employer-employee relationship. Concerns include the effect of unionization on salary and benefit expenditures, the erosion of management control on discipline, the potential intrusion of the union into the planning process, interference in establishing and reaching production goals, and even an emotional reaction to the "disloyal attitudes" of the employees who favor union representation. Since unions are a resource to which employees are entitled under law, the labor movement must be recognized and understood from historical and legal perspectives.

The seeds of the labor movement and labor legislation in the United States can be said to have been sown in the exploitive employment practices of the nineteenth and early twentieth century and nurtured both by the privations of the Depression and the insecurity of the aftermath.

The Industrial Revolution did more than change production methods; it reversed the economic base and social fiber of society. Individual producers and financial autonomy were replaced by a capitalist management–labor relationship in which the former unilaterally established the terms of employment. A good many of the new capitalist class developed a kind of "divine right" attitude from which flowed the abuses that have been described by historians, economists, sociologists, and even fiction writers: long hours, disproportionately low pay, harsh work rules, child labor, sweat shops, a disregard for safety, exploitation of immigrant groups, factory towns, company stores, arbitrary hiring and firing, and all the rest. Those conditions created the impetus for worker rebellion and unification. There followed years of labor-management confrontation marked by violence on both sides. A gradual strengthening of labor' position coupled with economic conditions led to the formation of permanent labor unions, government intervention, and finally the passage of worker-protective legislation.

Today, organized labor in the United States is a strong force both in the economy and the political arena. Union strikes can and have stopped production in multimillion dollar plants, closed down major school systems, disrupted transportation, sanitation, and other urban services, and shut down networks of coastal seaports. Union wage demands have made personnel expenditures the major item in many company budgets, and health and welfare programs have revolutionized benefit planning. Individual and companywide productivity, prices, public services, even the national balance of payments are affected by the agreements that labor negotiates. Presidential aspirants court labor's support. Labor actively lobbies for legislation to enact its programs, for example, the 1977 amendment increasing the federal minimum wage, the Trade Act of 1974, and ERISA.

When the labor movement began, it consisted of scattered groups operating in secrecy; by 1930 more than 3 million workers, 6 percent of the labor force, were unionized; in 1974 about 21.7 percent of the workforce or some 21,643,000 individuals were union members.* This transition and the development of current management-labor practices can be understood by considering the legislation regulating management-labor relations, organization procedures, the negotiating process, and contract administration.

LABOR AND THE LAW

There are two basic premises on which United States labor law is based. The first is that employees have the right to organize and the right to fair representation. The second is that commerce must be protected. Those two themes are repeated throughout the texts of major labor legislation both to explain the purpose

* U.S. Department of Labor, Bureau of Labor Statistics, Bulletin No. 1937, 1977.

of the law and to establish the jurisdictional prerogatives under which Congress has acted.

Legislation

Five pieces of legislation serve as landmarks in federal labor law: the Railway Labor Act (1926), the Federal Anti-Injunction Act (1932), the National Labor Relations Act (1935), the Labor Management Relations Act (1947), and the Labor Management Reporting and Disclosure Act (1959). In addition to setting the guidelines for employer-employee union relations, taken in sequence, the laws provide an insight into the history of the labor movement as well as public perception of labor and management.

RAILWAY LABOR ACT. Although limited to railways, the Railway Labor Act was a milestone because it established the pattern of future labor legislation. The stated purpose of the Act was to protect the public from the effects of labor disputes in an industry vital to the public welfare. The thrust of the law was the recognition of the right of employees to organize and the obligation of the railways to engage in collective bargaining with employees and/or their representatives. In addition, the Act created a Railway Adjustment Board and a National Mediation Board to administer the law and assist in settling disputes.

FEDERAL ANTI-INJUNCTION ACT. The Norris-La Guardia Act, as it is known, described the individual employee as powerless to affect the terms of his employment, confirmed his right to organize, and severely restricted the use of court injunctions by employers as a means of countering labor disputes. The law provided that injunctions could be issued only after a hearing and then only if management could establish that employees were engaged in illegal activities, that irreparable damage to property would result, or that law enforcement agencies were unable to provide protection to property. It also established that no organization could be held liable for the actions of individual members unless collusion could be proved.

NATIONAL LABOR RELATIONS ACT. Also known as the Wagner Act, the National Labor Relations Act extended the principles of the Railway Labor Act to employers and employees engaged in interstate commerce. It reiterates the premise that employees who are not organized are at a disadvantage because they have neither the resources nor the prerogatives enjoyed by management under the corporate structure. In addition to establishing the employees' right to organize and the employer's obligation to bargain, it created the National Labor Relations Board, outlined a procedure for the Board to review complaints, invested the Board with investigatory and enforcement powers, and affirmed the employees' right to strike.

LABOR MANAGEMENT RELATIONS ACT. The Taft-Hartley Act, as the Labor Management Relations Act is commonly known, is significant in that it not only reaffirmed employees' rights and management's responsibilities but also recognized that unions can have a discernible effect on commerce and employees' prerogatives. The law defined and outlined unfair labor practices by both employers and unions, imposed specific restraints on the activities of both, and required labor to maintain a reporting relation with the Secretary of Labor. The National Labor Relations Board was expanded and its activities detailed. Unions were prohibited from making political contributions; labor unions were declared able to sue and be sued; secondary boycotts were prohibited; and the right of states to legislate against union shops was affirmed.

LABOR MANAGEMENT DISCLOSURE ACT. An outgrowth of investigations into financial practices and abuses within some unions and the questionable relationships between certain employers and labor organizations, the Labor Management Disclosure Act was designed to protect the rights of union members. It requires that specific reports detailing the financial affairs of unions be filed with the Secretary of Labor, requires audits of union funds, and provides for the active participation of the membership in electing union officials and conducting union business. It requires management to report the use of consultants hired to influence employees in the exercise of their rights and the receipt of monies from labor organizations.

SUMMARY. Although subsequent amendments have extended coverage and precedents have been set by National Labor Relations Board rulings and court decisions, the above legislation, with Taft-Hartley as the dominant force, has established the framework of management-labor relations. Its thrust can be summarized as follows:

1. Employees have the right to form collective bargaining units; employers must recognize unions that meet established criteria.
2. Employers and unions must recognize employees' rights, bargain in good faith, and refrain from engaging in unfair labor practices.
3. Commerce must be protected from disruptions caused by the actions of employers and/or unions.
4. The National Labor Relations Board is the watchdog of both labor and management.

National Labor Relations Board

Because the National Labor Relations Board (NLRB) exerts a powerful influence in labor relations, it is helpful to understand its organization and functions.

The Board itself is composed of five members appointed by the President for five-year terms that are staggered to provide continuity of tenure. The Board is supported in its Washington, D.C., headquarters by a General Counsel and technical staff assigned to each board member. Key to the operations are the regional offices, which are assigned authority for pertinent labor activities within specified geographic areas.

The regional offices are the focus of much of the Board's activities, since they bear the responsibility for the bulk of the day-to-day interaction with the Board's various publics. That includes overseeing union elections, certifying employee representatives, and reviewing charges of unfair labor practices. In general, the regional office reviews, investigates, and makes the decisions in those areas and then refers the case and evidence to the Board for possible review and finalization of the decision.

The Board has full powers to investigate matters brought to its attention and to enforce its decisions. A regional office may subpoena witnesses, records, and other evidence, take depositions, examine witnesses, and so on. Although proceedings are similar to those found in a courtroom, the thrust is more toward fact-finding and the Trial Examiner takes a more active role than the courtroom judge in examining witnesses, the presentation and requisition of evidence, and the like. The Board in turn has the power to obtain court enforcement of its rulings.

Unfair Labor Practices

One of the most far-reaching provisions of the law is the prohibition of unfair labor practices. The clause is designed to allow the processes that fall within the scope of the law to be carried out in as free an atmosphere as is possible, and especially to protect the rights of the worker.

Hence it is an unfair labor practice for an employer to interfere in any way with his employees' right to organize. He cannot use coercion, restraints, threats, or promises to dissuade employees from organizing, nor can he discriminate against an employee who favors a union. Neither may an employer engage in illegal practices to uncover information about the union or proclivities of workers or refuse to bargain with the certified representative(s) of his workers. No employer may dominate or seek to dominate a union or make illegal payments to or receive them from a union. Thus the law outlaws specific employer activities including the use of yellow-dog contracts and blacklists, moving or threatening to move to avoid unionization, spying on employees, implementing new wage-benefit programs during an organization attempt, favoring one union over another, firing or refusing to promote employees because of their pro-union activities, withholding normal benefits or privileges from pro-union workers, and similar practices.

Unions, on the other hand, are forbidden to threaten or coerce either workers or employers. Secondary boycotts, illegal strikes or picketing, substantial payments to employers and/or their representatives, and receipt of illegal monies from employees are prohibited. No union may refuse to bargain in good faith with an employer.

If an unfair labor practice is committed or thought to have been committed, a charge is filed with the regional office of the NLRB by employee, employer, or union. The regional office reviews the claims and, if there is a reasonable basis for the charge, files a complaint against the offending party, who must respond within ten days. Failure to answer such a complaint results in a judgment against the complainant. If the accused party denies the complaint, a trial examiner is appointed to conduct a formal hearing and render a judgment. The judgment with all the evidence and testimony then is filed with the Board and becomes a ruling if all is in order and no appeals are made.

If the judgment is contested, the Board reviews the case and makes a ruling. Further appeals to a U.S. District Court are possible.

Once a ruling has been made, the Board has the power, if necessary, to obtain a court order to enforce the judgment. Thus, if the Board finds that an employer has unfairly fired a worker for union activities, a court order can be obtained to insure that the individual is rehired with back pay.

THE ORGANIZING PROCESS

Perhaps the most traumatic and eye-opening confrontation between union and employer comes during the organizing attempt. The situation is rife with emotionalism and calls for a thorough understanding of issues and rights. If the employer intends to oppose unionization, a focus on union strategy and some well-planned counterstrategy are in order.

The Union Thrust

Although unions sometimes are approached by employees, it is more usual for union organizers to make the initial contact. It is their business to keep informed about likely prospects, either individual employers or industries with personnel practices or problems that foster worker dissatisfaction. Their aims are first to convince workers that a union will be an effective spokesman in convincing management that it should correct the perceived injustices and then to win a majority of the potential bargaining unit.

To sell the employees, the union strategy usually begins with a general issue and becomes more specific as the organizers learn about on-the-job occurrences. At that point they will create or develop specific issues based on real incidents to portray management as interested only in profits and therefore as naturally indifferent to the welfare of the worker. At the same time the union will be depicted as caring about the individual. That kind of "us against them" approach is designed to foster a worker-union identification and will carry an emotional as well as rational appeal.

A classic example of such union strategy occurred during an organization campaign against a nursing home in which there were real personnel problems: failure of management to com-municate, insufficient aide training, and generally poor super-visory practices. The emotional crisis of the campaign came when a pro-union aide depicted a director of nursing as order-ing her to treat a patient with a sore running with pus even though the aide was certain to carry the deadly infection home to her baby. In fact there was a patient with a running sore, and a culture of the sore had been negative. If the aide had been properly drilled in sanitation techniques; if the charge nurse had supervised the procedures more closely; and if the director of nursing had shown some concern, reviewed proper techniques for safe patient contact, and then communicated the result of the culture, there would have been no major issue and the dra-matics could have been avoided. As it was, the aide, who sin-cerely perceived herself to have been victimized, was an emo-tional bomb and a considerable amount of firefighting was necessary to restore equilibrium not only among the aides but in other departments as well.

Procedurally, the union organizers will begin by informally sounding out individual employees or by distributing prop-aganda usually in or near the premises—parking lots and employee entrances—and holding individual conversations. This is usually followed by holding a meeting at which union officials will address workers with an emotional pitch designed to get as much audience involvement and response as possible. The next step is to solicit signatures on a petition or, more typically, on union enrollment cards.

Once 30 percent of a potential bargaining unit signs enroll-ment cards, a petition can be filed with the regional office of the NLRB. That office will review the petition and, if all is in order, supervise a certification election. If a majority of employees in the potential bargaining unit vote in favor of representation, the union is certified and the employer must enter into collective bargaining; if a majority vote against union representation, unionization is averted and no further organizing attempts or picketing can be conducted for 12 months. (When neither alter-native receives a majority, a run-off election will be held. If more than one union is involved and there is no antiunion majority, a run-off election between unions may be scheduled.)

A key issue in union strategy is the determination of the bargaining unit. To begin with, certain legal restraints are involved, since the Labor Management Relations Act requires that there be some occupational commonality among members of a bargaining unit. Thus professionals cannot be in the same bargaining unit with clerical personnel and service workers, and security guards must be excluded from bargaining units with nonsecurity personnel. Beyond such restraints it is to the union's advantage from the perspectives of economics and leverage to include the greatest possible number of employees in the bargaining unit. But since organizers must be realistic about their prospects, they may limit themselves initially to organizing only the portion of the workforce that is most likely to vote for union representation. For instance, they might concentrate on service workers in the initial organization effort and attempt to add clerical workers at a later date.

One additional point should be made. Both management reaction and timing are important elements in union strategy. If management reaction is weak, the union may attempt to persuade the employer to accept the union without contest and thereby eliminate the need for an election. If an election is necessary, timing is important. Since losing an election not only will involve loss of prestige but also will constrain activities for one year, the union will schedule NLRB petitions and picketing campaigns carefully. The strategy will be to delay the petition until it can be sure of a majority vote, and not just the 30 percent necessary to secure an election. The same principle applies to picketing, since the law requires that picketing be discontinued after 30 days if no election is held. This means that, after 30 days, the union must either petition NLRB or stop picketing. At that point the employer, who is sure that he will win the election, has an option to petition NLRB and potentially halt the union drive.

Employer Response

Not every union organization attempt suceeeds. In some instances employee response to union overtures is so negative that organizers withdraw after a brief reconnaissance. In other situations, even after a concerted effort, the union suspends activity because it cannot be reasonably sure of securing a majority vote. Sometimes unions even lose elections.

The employer opposing the union campaign must plan his strategy with equal care and a good deal of objectivity. The first step is to assess resources and vulnerability; then a comprehensive plan of response must be outlined.

SELF-ASSESSMENT. Once the decision to resist unionization has been made, it is necessary to assess the resources of the organization to determine whether outside help is needed. Both the size of the threat and the extent of in-house expertise are considerations. Several questions must be addressed.

The first question is whether the workforce is likely to be receptive to union overtures. The overall morale of the workforce, the nature of complaints, turnover, and general observations of key people will provide an initial impression. But perhaps the best source will be first-line supervisors, who have the closest and least formal contact with employees. In surveying opinion it is imperative to stress the need for frankness. If people report what they think the questioner wants to be told rather than facts, the cost could be considerable.

The next question is the dollar cost of unionizing the potential bargaining unit. The size of the unit is one factor, and the amount of potential settlement is another. Other employers in the area whose employees are members of the union in question can provide pertinent information. There are two cost factors beyond the initial settlement: whether the bargaining unit is likely to be expanded at a later date and whether wages and benefits will have to be increased for nonunion employees either to maintain equity or dissuade those employees from seeking union representation at a later time.

As to in-house expertise, two issues arise. The first consideration is the necessity to avoid unfair labor practices. It is essential that the individual spearheading the campaign be familiar enough with labor legislation to avoid such pitfalls and make sure that union organizers do not engage in such practices themselves. Although legal training is not required, a basic understanding of the law and sense enough to consult expert sources such as the NLRB compliance officer are necessary. The second factor is the availability of an individual with the intrapersonal and communications skills necessary to sell management's message to employees. It also is essential that such a person have the time to devote to the assignment.

The decision then becomes an exercise of judgment and priorities. Does the potential gain—an increased chance of winning the union election—justify the expense involved in retaining expert assistance? Or to reverse the question, is the potential cost of a union settlement great enough to require outside assistance?

CAMPAIGN STRATEGY. Employer strategy is not unlike that used by union organizers. The first step is to gather as much information as possible on the causes of employee dissatisfaction, the strength of union support, the reasons for employee opinion, and the issues raised by the union. Again the emphasis must be on developing accurate information, since facts must support management's communications to employees.

There should be a review of the wage-and-benefit structure, personnel policies, training, safety, time-off and scheduling systems, discipline, and the basic atmosphere of employee relations with a particular emphasis of supervisory competence. Recent changes in work procedures, grievance issues, turnover statistics and trends, and grapevine rumors should all be examined. Such information will allow management to anticipate the issues and charges likely to be raised by the union and be able to either refute them or put them into the appropriate perspective. That can be done only if management is willing to be objective and self-critical.

It is also advisable to assess the strength of the competition and to know what issues the union is stressing as well as the phase to which the campaign has advanced. Although there are legal restraints against "spying" on employees and management attendance at union meetings, it is permissible to ask questions openly as long as there is no intent to coerce, discriminate, or punish. Again, supervisors are a likely source of such information.

The next step is to design a response to be communicated to employees. Just as the union has the right to criticize management, so the employer has the specific right to express opinion, criticize union positions on tactics, and disseminate other information to employees orally, graphically, or in writing. It is imperative that no communication contain a hint of threat, coercion, or promise of reward. Therefore, it is advisable that managers avoid discussing the union issue in private conversations with single employees. It is better to conduct any such discussions in public areas with several persons present.

Written material stating management's opinion of the union and preference for avoiding a third-party intrusion into the employer-employee relationship can be disseminated. A synopsis of existing employee benefits and the employer-borne cost may be publicized. It is often a good tactic to hold informal meetings with small groups to discuss the issues and throw the floor open for questions. But no promises may be made, no benefits added, and no new wage plan implemented.

Although there is no legal constraint on criticizing the union or its tactics, restraint should be used. Wholesale criticism may produce a negative effect, especially in a geographic area in which unions are popular. To criticize a union to employees whose families are union members is nonproductive. To slander unions to people who have been brought up to regard a union as a friend is foolish. If the union is vulnerable to attack, it is better to publicize documented information regarding union actions: union settlements with other employers that are less favorable than current conditions, a history of increases in union dues, and so on.

Many employers have responded to union attack by conceding that union criticism is legitimate but denying that the presence of a union will eliminate the problems. Such an admission usually is followed by an expression of willingness to work for solutions and a preference that a direct dialogue be established between employees and management without the interference of a third party. That approach *must* be taken by stressing that it is an *opinion* and *preference* that the relationship can be improved without a third party—no promises, no threats, no coercion, no unfair labor practices!

As disseminators of information and management opinion and as sources of information, supervisors can play a key role in any antiunion campaign. To maximize their value, management must make a serious effort to keep them informed about campaign plans and developments. It is also crucial that they be trained to handle employee inquiries effectively and, especially, avoid committing unfair labor practices. They should be consulted regularly in groups or individually, particularly if union sympathy in their departments is pronounced.

Because it is also important to prevent additional issues from arising during an organization attempt, it is necessary to work closely with supervisors on discipline problems. It may be advisable to set up a discipline review system as a safeguard to avoid crises and situations in which a prounion employee may receive questionable discipline.

One other point should be made: the right of the employer to limit the union's access to employees. Under normal circumstances union organizers have the right to approach employees only in public areas. Ordinarily, they need not be granted access to work sites, other areas normally closed to the public, or even the employer's property. Prounion employees, naturally, can pursue union activity on employer-owned property including restricted areas such as cafeterias and locker rooms; but they can be restrained when such activities interfere with work, provided there is no harassment or unusual restriction.

Decertification

Just as employees have the right to organize, so they have the right to withdraw their consent to union representation. The employer, in such a case, must limit his involvement to providing information on the employee's right to petition for union decertification and the procedures to be followed.

Thirty percent or more of the employees in a bargaining unit may petition a regional office of NLRB for an NLRB election. If a majority of employees vote to withdraw from the union, the union is decertified. Any promises, threats, or other coercions by the employer are considered unfair labor practices. Open communications are permitted on the same basis as in organization attempts.

THE NEGOTIATING PROCESS

Once the NLRB has certified a union as the representative of employees within a bargaining unit, the employer is obligated to enter into collective bargaining to negotiate an agreement governing terms of employment. The agreement will remain in force for a specified length of time, usually two or three years, after which a new agreement will be negotiated. Whether the bargaining involves an initial or renegotiated contract, there are three areas of concern: the postures of the negotiating parties, negotiating procedures, and the scope of the agreement.

Negotiating Postures

The roles of management and labor and the negotiating posture that each party assumes are colored by the organizing process, the hostility of the campaign, management's basic philosophy toward the management-union relationship, and the relative strengths and weaknesses of the two parties and the team members.

In the final analysis, the employer is at the negotiating table because he is obliged to be there. The union representatives are there because they have won the first round—the certification election—by convincing bargaining unit employees that the union will be able to win better terms of employment. In addition, the inclusion of union stewards or some members of the rank and file on the negotiating committee reinforces the expectation that the union will assume the role of the aggressor— "demanding" that its terms be met.

However, there are other factors involved. One is management's attitude toward the union. Management may aim to confront the union, to subvert union influence, and, if possible, to destroy the union; on the other extreme is the management approach of forming a kind of partnership in which the union is involved in much of the corporate planning. Although most employers take a more moderate approach, their position within the spectrum between confrontation and partnership will affect the tenor of negotiations. The relative strength of the personalities on the respective negotiating teams will have a similar influence on the proceedings.

But beyond the philosophical and personal factors there are realities of strength versus weakness in the basic positions the respective parties will assume. The size of the bargaining unit, the size and resources of the union, the financial position of the employer, previous agreements within an industry, the overall economic milieu, all will impact negotiations. Normally, the employer will try to give away as little as possible while the union attempts to achieve a liberal settlement. But the union must deal with reality. It is not to its advantage to insist on terms that will result in the employer's going out of business, in layoffs or other staff reductions, or in a work stoppage, particularly if no strike fund has been established.

Negotiating Procedures

Generally, negotiations are conducted by two teams. Each team has a chief negotiator, who is authorized to make definite commitments, as well as several other members. The union team will include several of the rank-and-file membership, generally stewards, and one or two experts such as business representatives or technical advisers. Management usually includes on its team technical advisers with expertise in such fields as wage-and-salary administration or benefits and a line manager. A labor lawyer or consultant also may assist management, particularly in the case of the employer with little or no experience in such areas.

The entire negotiating team from each side usually attends the initial sessions. When large corporations and unions or complex issues are involved, there may be subcommittees to work on isolated issues. But the hard bargaining in later stages often is conducted by one or two people from each side—sometimes in informal and/or off-the-record meetings.* The full team is brought together for the formal offer and acceptance of terms and the signing ceremony. The contract is then submitted to the union membership, and perhaps a committee of union officials, for ratification.

The process itself typically begins with the union's presentation of its demands, often prior to the opening of formal negotiations. That tends to be a long list compiled by the leadership with some contributions by the rank and file. The demands will include issues intended to be the main areas of the sessions, minor points more likely to be handled administratively than contractually, and some that are designed to be trade-offs or feelers for demands which union leaders anticipate will be the meat of future agreements.

Some management negotiators limit themselves to dealing with the demands drawn up by the union. Others prepare their

* The informal settings in which some of these agreements are made traditionally have included rest rooms. That practice has become more complicated with the passage of "sunshine laws" requiring full disclosure of negotiations that involve government monies and the inclusion of women on negotiating teams.

own counterproposals. In some instances the counterproposals are designed to be bases of discussion; in others they represent management's "final offer." The latter posture, which is taken when management adopts a more aggressive stance, requires much planning and an experienced team. If the counterproposals are publicized, there is a danger of committing an unfair labor practice.

The first session usually is devoted to logistics. After initial arrangements have been made—times and location of meetings, payment of union stewards on the committee, other expense items, seating arrangements, and similar procedural matters— the real work of the negotiations gets under way. Ordinarily the demands are presented formally and discussed so that there is a mutual understanding of terms. Although that may seem to be a minute point, it is essential to management not only to reach a mutual understanding of the issue but to insure that the contract language will be clear and unambiguous to prevent misinterpretation to one party's advantage during the life of the contract.

In the early phases of the process the less substantive issues, including clarification of language from the expiring contract, may be discussed. At this point the trading begins as the parties either accept or reject the other demands or effect compromises. The give and take usually continues until the less difficult problems have been eliminated and the way is cleared for negotiators to concentrate on the main issues. Isolation of issues brings about the hard negotiating in which the principal negotiators assume their more dominant position and the adjunct members of the team become less active.

The negotiations will result in a comprehensive agreement that will define the terms of employment for the life of the contract. It will include such details as a description of the bargaining unit, the duration of the contract, a commitment to begin negotiations for a new agreement before the lapse of the current contract, membership enrollment procedures, check-off systems for collection of dues, and a provision that union membership be required for all permanent employees hired for the bargaining unit.

Sections will be devoted to compensation, including revised salary scales reflecting general wage settlements and, if applicable, longevity increases for individual employees. Employee contributions to benefit programs and/or union welfare funds will be described, as will time-off benefits. All matters relating to employment terms will be listed, including wash-up or preparation time, scheduling and duration of breaks, uniform requirements, and payment arrangements. Pay periods and pay days, job-posting systems, in some cases hiring procedures, and the rights and duties of union stewards will be incorporated.

Two clauses that merit special attention are those defining management rights and seniority. Since good order requires that management retain broad powers to plan and regulate the activities and financial aspects of the organization, labor agreements contain specific clauses delineating those rights. Employers generally prefer a management rights clause that will give them the broadest powers possible.

The other issue with far-reaching repercussions is seniority. If the seniority clause is written in a way that allots seniority in the bargaining unit as a whole rather than within work units or departments, layoffs and other work reduction measures will require interdepartmental bumping (the practice of having workers with more seniority replace those with less, even in lower-paying jobs) and possibly necessitate a major training effort.

Another ramification of seniority lies in the promotion and job-bidding procedures. Since the union's philosophy typically will recognize length of service rather than performance variables, union negotiators will favor a system of promotions and transfer under which workers will be moved into such positions solely on the basis of seniority. It may be to management's advantage to qualify such clauses to emphasize qualifications and work records and make seniority a tertiary consideration.

ADMINISTERING THE AGREEMENT

The philosophies that color the negotiating encounter between management and the union will affect the attitudes with which the two parties will interact during the life of the contract. Beyond that the existence of an agreement and presence of the union will significantly change the relations between employers and employees. In place of the loose employment agreement that exists when an individual is offered and accepts a given job at a specified wage with whatever hours and benefits might be discussed in the employing process, there is a legal document that describes in minute detail the terms that bind employer *and* employee. There are procedures, schedules, and third-party representation with little room for give and take. However, it is appropriate to keep the roles of all the parties in the three-way relationship in perspective.

The workforce has impacted the relationship significantly. It has elected representatives to act on its behalf; it has advised those representatives of the needs and priorities to be considered in the bargaining process; it has ratified the agreement. That participation makes the workforce an active party in the determination of the employment milieu but does not change its role as producer of the goods and/or services provided by the organization.

The union's responsibility is twofold—to act as agents for employees in the bargaining process and to insure that employee contractual rights are observed. That means the union represents the entire workforce in securing acceptable terms of employment and individual workers in the pursuit of their rights under the established agreement. It has no other prerogatives. Union officials cannot interject themselves into the management, supervisory, or production process in any other capacity.

Management maintains the responsibility for running the organization, establishing long- and short-term goals, and devising work methods and protocols (provided they do not violate the contract), financial management, work assignments, and the like. It is restricted only by the terms of the contract and federal legislation, including prohibitions against unfair labor practices. It must consult with the union only when its plans will impact the employment terms established by the contract, as when insurance coverage is added or changed or a job held by a union member is eliminated or altered. Management does have the prerogative to consult the union in any matter that potentially will affect union employees: departmental organization, employment referral, implementation of federal safety regulations, and so on.

It is important to communicate those roles to supervisors in order to reaffirm the supervisors' place in the organization, their prerogatives in production areas, and their responsibilities in employee relations. Supervisors also must be given a thorough indoctrination in the terms of the agreement and the new systems and procedures precipitated by the contract. If there has not been a grievance procedure, in-depth training in handling grievances is in order. If poor supervisory practices contributed to unionization, it may be advisable to develop a training program to rectify matters, if only to minimize the number of grievances likely to be pursued.

Beyond those roles and relationships, unionization necessitates certain changes in procedures and systems including employment practices, compensation, and employee relations. Employment practices will be altered most radically if there is a requirement to hire through union halls, as is the practice in certain of the building trades and on the docks. More likely, there will be a requirement to post jobs within the bargaining unit so that current employees may have preference for jobs or shift assignments.

Depending on the terms of the contract (see the preceding discussion), seniority will be a factor in such transactions. One complication that should be considered is the potential ramification of such transfers. Is there a new probationary period? If a new work unit or department is involved, how will work seniority be affected? If a transferee fails in the new job, will he have to be transferred back to his previous job, possibly bumping another person? If he is transferred back, how will his fellow workers react to him? Those questions are posed not to deter such transfers or promotions but to point out the need to anticipate problems and develop policies and possibly counseling resources prospectively.

With respect to compensation, the first major change often is cost. The second might be the union thrust to pay all workers the same rate for the same work, perhaps with a small differentiation to recognize longevity, but with no correlation between performance and increments. Fitting employees into the new wage scale may have its own complications. The problem will be minimized if there is a substantial change in the starting rate or if current wages tend to be clustered closely. If there are employees whose pay rates are above the settlement, there is a problem. Should they be red-circled and receive whatever longevity raises are due them? Or should their wages be frozen until the rest of the workforce catches up with them? If longevity increases are included in the settlement, should current employees receive wage adjustments reflecting length of service, or will everyone be placed at the new starting wage rate? If there is a provision to negotiate an additional interim increase to reflect rises in the cost of living, how can those sums be budgeted? If employees are to be covered under union health and welfare programs, will any employees, particularly older workers, lose benefits?

The process of employee relations will be affected in three ways: the role of union stewards and business agents, the increased importance of progressive discipline and documentation, and the extension of the grievance procedure to include arbitration. The introduction of the union steward and business agent into employer-employee communications is a major alteration in that relationship. Employees not only will bring complaints to the attention of union stewards but will usually elect to have stewards join them in the pursuit of grievances. Likewise, generalized complaints may be brought to the attention of the business agent, who also may be consulted about grievances, particularly if the grievance reaches an advanced step or if drastic discipline has been initiated. Thus the employer must interact not only with individual employees but with employee representatives as well. The very presence of additional people tends to make such proceedings more formal and eliminates the possibility of off-the-record discussion.

Since employee representatives are likely to be consulted by employees subject to discipline, there is an increased need to use a progressive system of discipline and to emphasize the importance of objective documentation (see Chapter 5). If there has been no grievance system, supervisors and middle managers will have to be trained in grievance handling.

In any case the grievance system will be expanded to include outside arbitration of disputes that cannot be settled between the employer and union. The arbitration process requires the retaining of an independent arbitrator (or in complex cases, a panel), acceptable to both parties, who conducts a formal hearing, examines the evidence and testimony of witnesses, and makes a judgment that both union and employer are bound to accept. Arbitrators are individuals with backgrounds in labor relations; often they are members of the academic community. Generally there is a pool of arbitrators within a geographic area who can be called upon to settle disputes. Ordinarily the expense of retaining an arbitrator is shared by union and employer.

PREVENTIVE MEDICINE

Employers who wish to avoid unionization would be well advised to consider why employees seek to organize. As has been noted, unions have their origins in exploitive employment practices that breed worker dissatisfaction and alienation. Although it is impossible to create a utopian work situation, it is possible to provide a work environment in which employees do not feel the need to seek external assistance. As discussed throughout this book, that means the development of adequate personnel policies, fair work standards, good supervisory practices, the opportunity for personal and professional development, fair compensation, the elimination of arbitrary employment practices, and a good communications system. Whenever possible, employees should be involved in the development of the policies and systems that will affect them. Having them complete job questionnaires for wage-and-salary programs, using opinion surveys, utilizing grievance and suggestion systems, and providing information, explanation, and rationale will give the workforce a sense of participation and identification with the organization.

Beyond those internal considerations, keeping abreast of union activity in the community never hurts, especially for the employer in a targeted industry. In many areas employers form associations within their industries to exchange information on union organizing attempts, the campaign issues, demands, settlement terms, employee reactions, and the like. In some instances these associations provide members with technical assistance or expert consultation in antiorganization campaigns or negotiations.

INDEX

Other Small Business Books from AMACOM...

Legal Handbook for Small Business

Marc J. Lane

A Main Selection of the McGraw-Hill Management Book Guild

"Extraordinary...an easy-to-read and absolutely essential book for the head of any small business." **Boardroom Reports**

"Recommended" **Library Journal**

Written in your kind of language by a practicing attorney.   **$14.95**

Small Business Works!

How to Compete and Win in the Free Enterprise System

Eugene L. Gross, Adrian R. Cancel, and Oscar Figueroa

"Small business success is not easily had, but with this book you can get a running start. Recommended to budding entrepreneurs." **SSC Booknews.**

"Designed to help people in business understand the mechanics of business operation and the interrelationships of operational units." **Houston Business Journal**

$14.95

Successful Small Business Management

Leon A. Wortman

A Selection of the McGraw-Hill Management Book Guild

"Provides the basic organizational management, accounting, and marketing techniques...to launch a small business. A concise, practical guide which offers the necessary techniques and experiences in a comprehensive fashion." **Booklist**

$12.95

Financial Management for Small Business

Edward N. Rausch

A Selection of the McGraw-Hill and Macmillan Book Clubs

This book gives you the protection you need when dealing with accountants, bankers, lawyers, partners, and suppliers. It shows you how to measure their performance and use them to your advantage. And it deals with practical ways to cut risks and improve your chances for survival and success!   **$12.95**

A Division of American Management Associations
135 West 50th Street, New York, N.Y. 10020

0-8144-5509-3